T0042907

THE WILL TO SEE

Also by Bernard-Henri Lévy

The Virus in the Age of Madness

The Empire and the Five Kings: America's Abdication and the Fate of the World

The Genius of Judaism

Public Enemies: Dueling Writers Take on Each Other and the World (with Michel Houellebecq)

Left in Dark Times: A Stand against the New Barbarism

American Vertigo: Traveling America in the Footsteps of Tocqueville

War, Evil, and the End of History

Who Killed Daniel Pearl?

Sartre: The Philosopher of the Twentieth Century

Adventures on the Freedom Road: The French Intellectuals in the 20th Century

The Testament of God

Barbarism with a Human Face

THE WILL TO SEE

Dispatches from a World of Misery and Hope

Bernard-Henri Lévy

Yale
UNIVERSITY PRESS
NEW HAVEN & LONDON

English translation by Steven B. Kennedy.

Yale University Press books may be purchased in quantity for educational, business, or promotional use. For information, please e-mail sales.press@yale.edu (U.S. office) or sales@yaleup.co.uk (U.K. office).

Designed by Dustin Kilgore.
Set in Yale New and Alternate Gothic types by Integrated Publishing Solutions.
Printed in the United States of America.

Library of Congress Control Number: 2021937089
ISBN 978-0-300-26055-7 (hardcover : alk. paper)

A catalogue record for this book is available from the British Library.

This paper meets the requirements of ANSI/NISO Z39.48-1992 (Permanence of Paper).

10 9 8 7 6 5 4 3 2 1

CONTENTS

INTRODUCTION

Reporting . . .

The first thought this word always brings to mind is *universel reportage* and the disdain in which France's most exacting poet held it.

For I belong to a generation that viewed Stéphane Mallarmé (1842–1898) – the aristocratic poet who detonated the prose of the coming twentieth century – as one of its most incandescent masters.

I was twenty years old when the author of *Vers et Prose* joined the band of "theoretical anti-humanists" who, with their proclivity for grand thought, their fetish for science and pure criticism, their love of a language already too heavy with mysteries to weigh itself down with those of the world, seemed to reject "taking the side of things," the worship of "native soil," and, to speak like another poet, Victor Hugo (whom Mallarmé called "Mr. Verse"), the religion of "seen things."

And the idea of putting language to a use other than literature, the idea that it might leave the pure, breathless space where "nothing takes place but the place" – a role that Mallarmé famously assigned to the Book (the only bomb the poet knew of was the Book) – the idea of a literature of reality, wedded to the real and moving modestly to meet it – well, that idea did not sit well with my classmates and me, appearing as an affront to the lofty notions we held of words and their proper uses.

Of course, a text could be like the "devices" that the early anarchists, forerunners of the far left, had begun to explode, devices that Mallarmé felt lit up the world with a pale but persistent glow.

It could be, as it was for the surrealists interpreting Arthur Rimbaud in a manner unfailingly grandiose and exaggerated, the "white ray" falling from the sky to annihilate the human comedy. Or, as with Paul Valéry on his last visit to Mallarmé ("the pope of the Rue de Rome"), it could come at the "stroke of noon" to match "fireworks" with "silence replete with dizziness and dealing."

But we left to others the triviality of real things, the humble task of observing them, of traveling to the four corners of the earth under the most inhospitable circumstances, and of trapping the concrete and true (the truth of names and faces, not the version that triumphs today in digital illusions and their data tracks). We left to others the challenge of striking out and seizing wars at their most messy, suffering at its most unthinkable, and fleeting details that capture destinies bound for insignificance. In short, the simple, ordinary, and ugly immediacy of seemingly meaningless events seemed to us devoid of interest.

Why is that?

What more reason did I need at the time to turn quickly and decisively to reporting?

In making that personal choice, what possessed me to ignore

the counsel of those who believed my purpose in the world was to lead a life of words and thought?

Was it solely out of love for the United States that I ultimately chose Tom Wolfe, Truman Capote, Ernest Hemingway, Martha Gellhorn, and the "New Journalism" over "French theory"?

That is a question I have never asked myself.

I want to ask it here and now, on the threshold of this collection of pieces that appeared in French in *Paris Match,* the fine magazine that is also the consummate mass-circulation, mass-retail magazine of sensational human-interest stories, and in English in the world's leading business daily (the *Wall Street Journal*) – twin exemplars of Mallarmé's "universal reporting."

At my age, the time has come.

Though I have so far avoided the temptation to memorialize my years, and though I do not believe in acquired wisdom any more than in inexorable aging, it is time, to paraphrase Rimbaud, to recount the history of my follies.

PART ONE
MY CREED

1

THE ARCHAEOLOGY OF A REFLEX

First, there's a reflex.

I just said that I had never squarely posed the question of what led me to devote a big part of my life traveling the globe and bringing back stories.

But the truth is that I don't even pose the question in a practical way, on the run, with each new departure. I can set out for Eritrea, Bosnia, or Afghanistan; I can, as I did in 2020, take off for eight or nine destinations made even more inaccessible by health regulations and the great planetary lockdown, without taking the time to wonder, to weigh the pros and cons, or to ask myself, "What is motivating me? What makes me run? What leads me to throw myself once again into this mess or that inferno?"

Never any real hesitation.

Never any real fear, nor any special pride in not fearing.

Each time, a decision.

An opportunity and an intuition, followed by a decision.

And, confronted with glimpses, long ago, of the genocide in

Bangladesh, of the war in Tigray, or of the siege of Sarajevo; confronted with the scattered news reaching me today about the resurgence of ISIS menacing my friends in Iraqi Kurdistan; confronted with situations about which I either know nothing or have but a vague idea, such as the disaster in Darfur or the mutilated bodies of Christians in Nigeria or the featureless faces of villagers victimized by guerrillas in Burundi and Colombia—an inner compass provokes me to say, "No, impossible, intolerable; and what is most intolerable—disgusting, really—is the fierce indifference of my fellow Westerners."

It feels good to shed light on this reaction of mine.

For indeed, it is this true inner heart whose beating unfailingly sets my mind and body in motion.

Indeed, it is at the beckoning of this inner voice that I make my decisions and act on them.

To those who would ask what an inner voice might mean, I recommend reading Kant.

Or Pascal.

Or George Orwell and Upton Sinclair, whose irrefutable consciences speak to all hearts.

Or, earlier, Plato describing a Socrates inhabited from childhood by "a being half-divine" who, even when whispering, speaks more clearly than the grating voice of ready-made, resigned thinking.

Or Husserl seeing in the inner monologue, which he labeled the "solitary life of the soul," a truth not yet impaired by tactical concerns, compromises made so as to be understood, or the misunderstandings of bad faith.

To those who may be unconvinced or perplexed by this idea, to the skeptics who may laughingly declare that no one in this world could possibly give credence to such stories of original truth and inner morality; to the suspicious ones who may wink like Zarathustra's tarantulas while speculating about what inchoate desires, unavowed interests, or hidden motives might lie behind such a frank avowal of revolt against the scandal of evil—I concede that things are indeed more complicated. But that does not, at least in my eyes, cast doubt on the role of that pure and irrefutable voice, wordless but unwavering, always more persuasive than all of the lead-footed reasons for leaving things alone and not budging from one's spot.

A reflex is not immune to learning.

Nor is it immune to a collection of remembrances, old decisions, unforgettable friendships, mentors heeded, or books read and forgotten.

Nor to an inner cauldron whose chemical works can be broken down and reduced to their components, visible and invisible solvents and more or less active agents.

A reflex is not an immutable automatism, not a trick of the blood, and even less an instinct. It has a history from which it is always possible, with patience and probity, to discern the primal scene and its metamorphoses.

The archaeology of this reflex that led me time and again to leave my family and embrace the cause of a people not my own should not be very hard to reconstruct.

* * *

First, one would find strata common to the generation of men and women who were twenty years old in the late 1960s or early 1970s.

This was the puzzling time when, having just completed their

Latin compositions and their philosophy treatises, the most passionate young intellectuals dove headfirst into a Maoism that, while engendering many monstrosities of thought, had a beautiful motto: war on egotism—that is, against the timid, cowardly, and voracious ideas of His Majesty the Self.

It was for each of us the era—one might almost say the day—when we discovered on the main display table of the Paris bookshop Librairie La Joie de Lire, founded and operated by a valiant publisher by the name of François Maspero, a scathing, seething, incendiary book by Frantz Fanon, with a preface by Jean-Paul Sartre. *The Wretched of the Earth* was furiously dangerous while also inspired. I suppose I viewed as rhetorical excess the terrible dialectic of a revolt that promised to kill two birds with one stone: in shooting one European, the killer simultaneously eliminated one oppressor and another oppressed, leaving behind "one dead man and one free man." I am ashamed to admit that I did not truly understand these words as genuine calls for murder. I would have been very surprised to learn that they would later inspire the slogan "One Jew, One Bullet," proclaimed at the Durban conference. But that there were wretched masses on the earth, their wretchedness deriving not from the gods (the Old Testament God of my fathers had taught me, in a voice so low I was not aware of it, to spurn idolatry) but from their fellow man, from cultures, monarchies, tyrannies, oligarchies, and pseudo-democracies (unfailingly, I told myself, from gang leaders dressed up as priests)—*that* was the source of an anger that never left me, even as I distanced myself from Fanon and his book.

And then, serving as ballast against that initial anger, as a magnet on my compass, and as an inner voice that otherwise would have remained suspended without a mouthpiece, or worse, reduced to repeating the idiotic slogans of a nihilistic, murderous cell, there were some of the great professors mentioned in the introduction. In describing them as "anti-humanist," I left much unsaid.

They were indeed anti-humanist.

But now comes one of the amazing turns – one might even say "returns" – that important eras are not stingy in offering. This particular one has been little noted.

The same Jacques Lacan who had drowned the man of humanism in a bright forest of graphs and mathemes was also the one who exhorted each of us not to abandon our desire and its uniqueness as a speaking subject.

The same Michel Foucault who declared the death of man, "disappearing like a face drawn in sand on the shore," strove with equal assurance to defend the rights of real humans. Even better, in documenting the story of Pierre Rivière's parricide, reviving the memory of androgynous Herculine Barbin, and lending his voice to the prisoners in Attica or in the maximum-security wings of France's prisons, he did more than anyone to embrace the cause of real people, little people, invisible people, those whose names ring no bell, whom he saved from the ignominy of living and dying without glamour, reputation, dignity, or record.

And I can still hear Louis Althusser, the last time I saw him before my departure for Bangladesh. He was recommending me to his friend, economist Charles Bettelheim, under whom he thought I might do a doctoral dissertation. Althusser was standing at the entry of his office-apartment. Though I didn't know it at the time, he had just come from one of the electroshock sessions that were intended to treat the manic depression that was wearing him down. With a wild eye and a finger in the air, he looked at me and shouted: "People! Real people! Don't forget to talk to him about real people! Forgetfulness is our enemy!"

How was that possible? Did the distance between the two sides represent the difference between a metaphysics and regrets about it? Between despair and its remedy? Between a fundamental politics and a provisional one? Did it represent movement from one to the other? An error corrected (in the sense intended by Bachelard, whose epistemology was another major preoccupation, another source of inspiration, in those years)? Or had the concept of the person become richer over time? Were we to understand that the man of humanism – the overly simple and abstract concept of the individual that they all derided as a bag of wind, the man who stood not proudly as he did for the communists but instead rang hollow, hopelessly and ridiculously hollow – had been operating as an obstacle? And that by removing that obstacle, by looking behind the smokescreen of ideology, by digging, as after an avalanche, through the layer of chatter, sonorous illusions, and feeble thinking, we might rescue the flesh-and-blood people buried below?

I lean toward that hypothesis, though this is not the place to detail why.

What I will say here is that my masters' passion for pure thought, their Mallarméan idolatry of theory, their concepts so fanatically refined as to go missing, as the poet said, from the bouquet of the things of the world – all that had a paradoxical effect: ultimately it equipped us with a greater intelligence about the world, a concern for real things, a commitment to the very singular part that beings play, all made more compelling and urgent by the fact that we had previously been taught how to disengage ourselves from false thoughts and precritical illusions.

The archaeological excavation would then work its way through the phenomenal freedom – with one thing inducing another and the twirls of the masters inspiring more in their disciples – that our generation had with respect to higher education, degrees, and, soon enough, the careers that our "training" had brought our way: this freedom is so distant, when you think about it, from the tendency of today's young people to rush to be baptized into social and political life – that is, often enough, into the swamp.

My view is that the École Normale Supérieure on the Rue d'Ulm, the summit of academic excellence, shone with a bright light rarely seen. To be admitted, one had to be on familiar terms with Sophocles and Lucan, be able to decipher Homer without aid of translation, have read widely and deeply, and, over two or more years of intense cramming, have made oneself as poor in body as one wished to be rich in spirit.

But no sooner had we done this, no sooner had we entered this temple of knowledge, still haunted by the intimidating ghosts of Charles Péguy, Jean Jaurès, and Jean-Paul Sartre, than we were asked to exert an equal and opposite force to carry out an act of revolt for which I find no equivalent in the youth movements of today: to unjoin what we had just joined and, in effect, to scuttle our boats.

We had to forget the knowledge that had been crammed into us.

To throw into the fire our own notebooks and those of our books that Lacanian philosophy had taught us were the devil's spawn, no better than a slurry made from human misery, good only for prolonging the curse.

To imagine our garrets as red bases.

To look upon the indoor goldfish pond that Normaliens called the Basin of the Ernests as a meeting place of candidates for the great recantation.

To convert the school's historic cellars into laboratories for a crew of Gidean Lafcadios who, with pontifical seriousness, would deconstruct new thoughts or sometimes reconstruct them, always injecting enough obscurity to allow one to be very certain that they would remain gratuitous, would be of no possible use, and thus could not serve to enslave or enchant anyone at all.

To turn the lecture halls named for Dussane and Cavaillès into sites of memorable bedlam whenever Jean Beaufret, the favored disciple of the ex-Nazi Heidegger, took the stage.

And when we reached the last stage of our program, at the end of which we would receive the prestigious degree known as the *agrégation,* the rupture became even plainer. For just as we had latched on to the "Normale" in École Normale Supérieure as representing an abominable normalization process from which it was imperative to withdraw, so in the new distinction of the agrégation, acquired at great sacrifice and viewed by the older generations as a pedagogical and republican rite, we heard the word in its usual sense, its worst, dullest, and most brutal sense – that of knowledge aggregating, like mortar, into motionless matter, or that of a foul slurry hardening and sedimenting upon contact with airless knowledge.

Our professors, as I've said, were giants.

We had the example of Jacques Derrida and his invigorating commentary.

We had Michel Foucault, a virtuoso in the art of the trills, scales, and arpeggios of the music of dark worlds.

And we had Georges Canguilhem, older than those two, the

theorist of the normal and the pathological body, and thus of the question of death that the West had fatally adopted as its theme and that Canguilhem proceeded to classify, deploying the lucidity of a physician-philosopher and, like his own mentor, Jean Cavaillès, of a member of the Resistance motivated by "logic." Small, taciturn, and dry, Canguilhem was a classmate of Jean-Paul Sartre and a former commander of the anti-Nazi Resistance forces of Libération-Sud. We referred to him familiarly as "the Cang," but he was one of the totemic figures of Foucault's generation and my own. A quotation of his was the epigraph of *Cahiers pour l'Analyse*, the prestigious review founded by Jacques-Alain Miller, Jean-Claude Milner, François Régnault, and Alain Grosrichard at the Cercle d'Épistémologie of the École Normale. To his work I dedicated my 1969 master's thesis in philosophy.

But living life as an intellectual, surrounded by the four walls of aggregated concepts and thought, seemed to us like poison. And when, in 1794, the revolutionary National Assembly decreed the establishment of a new school – one that would bring together the most able professors from "all parts of the Republic" for the purpose of teaching the art of teaching in the cut-stone convent where Paris's museum of natural history was then housed – the face of the aggregated scholar it had in mind appeared to us the prototype of the servile technician that power always tries to attract: the face of the death of thought, the death of generosity, the death of life, and just plain death.

Some of us went to work in factories.

Others went to stir up revolution in Venezuela or Cuba.

For my part, I chose Bangladesh and the "Red Indies" where, for several months, I endeavored to support the birth of a nation.

And although not all of us pushed self-abnegation to these lengths, it was nevertheless a time when perhaps not the first reflex of a young graduate with heart, but certainly the second, bent in this direction: a spring – or more accurately a double spring – whose effect was to ensure that the more we had tasted of absolute knowledge, the more we had compressed the soul to make room for the gay and dismal sciences inhaled through a funnel to the point of drunkenness, well, the more fiercely we pulled away, leaving shame and glory behind to find the "things themselves" that we had earlier disdained.

It is useful to examine this mechanism.

First, to allow younger generations to inhale the scent of a radicalism that – despite its excesses and its having been touched by the wind whistling off the wings of scientism – had another aspect: it was animated by a preoccupation with the universal that is missing, I believe, from the ratiocinations of the "decolonial," race-based, difference-based, or narrow community-based thinking that holds sway among the far left of the twenty-first century.

Second, because at the very least we were seeking intellectual discomfort, a struggle with ourselves, a sense of intellectual divergence and debate that was not a threat to the self but essential for the construction of the mind – and these are the exact opposite of the coddled, comfortable "safe spaces" that so many of today's students insist on.

But most important because in that mechanism, that reflex, that pulling away, lay a singular intellectual merger in which the thirst for the absolute was all the stronger for having been wedded to an intimidating and demanding body of great thought, which, once stripped naked by its very disciples, simultaneously armed and emancipated them.

* * *

The other part of this story is more personal.

In a 1962 script that was to serve as the voice-over for his documentary film *Rage,* which took the form of a lyric journal, Pasolini writes, "Happy are the sons whose fathers were heroes."

Having met him a few times in the last years of his life, I know that Pasolini was aware that in saying this he was going against a romantic notion that dates, in France, from the opening pages of Alfred de Musset's *Confession of a Child of the Century.* The idea goes more or less like this: the misery of a generation of sons conceived under a "spotless sky" by colossal fathers who would "raise them to their gold-laced bosoms" where "shone all the glory" of the wars of the Revolution and the Empire; pity the young people stopped cold by progenitors – hussars, Old Guards, officers, uhlans – who, having been swept into service by the emperor, returned from their heroic adventures breathless, bloodied, and muddy, dogged by the same air of storm, tornado, lightning assaults, and epic defeats!

For Musset, the curse of the century was nothing more than being sentenced to repose by a father greater than oneself, to wondering about the snows of Moscow or the sun on the pyramids while listening to a constant refrain of "no more illusions; no more dreams of human greatness; all that's left in this world are pensions; become a priest!" Being a "lost generation" meant possessing an inherited strength that was now suddenly useless . . .

In my case, it was Pasolini who was right.

Indeed, I was lucky enough to be born of a father two times a hero.

The anti-Nazi Resistance: in mid-May 1944, he was with the First Division of the Free French forces, under the command of legendary general Diego Brosset and spearheading the Italy campaign. He was among those who scaled the steep ravines of mounts Faito and Majo to cover the Polish infantry, planting the French flag at the top of Monte Cassino and opening the way to the victory of the Allied forces.

Before that, however, he had enlisted in the international brigades in Spain, arriving in Barcelona the week he turned eighteen in July 1938 – still a boy – and returning several months later following the retreat from the Ebro front and the disbanding of his company. He went on to join the division that fought to the end, covering the *Retirada* in February 1939.

And I say that Pasolini got it right because I had those bold feats in mind when, in November 1971, having graduated from the École Normale Supérieure with a degree that gave me entrée to the professoriat, but determined to break away from the aestheticism of thought, from intellectual work of the professorial sort, and from cranking out books (a fate that struck me then as a dead end), I answered André Malraux's call when he proposed to form an international brigade for Bangladesh. I recounted our meeting in *Adventures on the Freedom Road.*

I say that Pasolini is right because even if my father, like all heroes, was reserved, these were the two great scenes present in our minds when, one Sunday nearly forty years later at our family's home in the country, I told him that I had suggested to Bosnian president Izetbegović the idea of leading an international brigade for Sarajevo. The president's response? "Do you know how to fight? Shoot? Drive a tank? No! Make a film instead, because a picture, when it's true, can be worth ten thousand guns." And my father's answer to that? After multiple admonitions, warnings, and gruff appeals to my sense of family responsibility, he decided that if I was going to make a documentary, I had best do it quickly and well, applying all the necessary means so that the result would be the least bad tribute to my new Catalonia. With that, he resolved to produce it, pulling in his respected business rival, tycoon and philanthropist François Pinault.

I cannot count how many times after his death (and even in some of the accounts collected here), I handled moments of weariness and doubt not by permitting myself to be paralyzed by the audacity of Musset's "old gray-haired army" but by mentally reciting these words of Diego Brosset, a fireproof quotation delivered in action on July 19, 1944, the day after the taking of Monte Cassino, and entered into my father's military record: "André Lévy, ambulance driver and stretcher bearer, always ready and willing, day or night, whatever the mission; carried out evacuations under mortar fire with total disregard for his own personal safety, returning several times to search for the wounded on lines then under intense enemy fire." These words give me courage. And they have been like a mysterious Ariadne's thread cast into the void of a climb in the Kurdish mountains or an open march at the Ukrainian front line . . .

To this magnificent heritage, which gave me so much strength, I must add details of some of my readings that were so alien to the tenor of the times that I did them somewhat clandestinely.

Malraux, obviously, whose name – like that of another writer, Romain Gary, Malraux's junior in every way, and whom I would also begin to see regularly – had become taboo, compromised by his association with Gaullist statism.

Sartre, hardly held in high regard except as a useful idiot and as a signatory, in *The Cause of the People,* of passages that are among the most indefensible of the Maoist leaders in France. But I was drunk on his nausea, on his "coalescing group," and, above all, on one of his ideas that I long held (and still do, deep down) as a sort of maxim: a bastard, a real one, is nothing other, metaphysically speaking, than a living being who conceives his own place on this earth, who does not doubt for an instant that this place is legitimately and eternally his, and who, consequently, will not budge from it for anything or anybody in the world.

And even *Don Quixote,* which I discovered in adolescence through the Schlegel brothers, Ludwig Tieck, and the German Romantics, who were the only ones not to have ridiculed or parodied the idealistic hidalgo. I do not know if many people still read *Don Quixote.* No more, probably, than read Malraux's *Man's Fate,* Lawrence's *The Seven Pillars of Wisdom,* Hemingway's *For Whom the Bell Tolls,* or any other book capable of pulling them out, however briefly, from the endless collection of faces, hardly more individualized than flies or ants, that seems to have become the resigned ideal of a large portion of humanity in the era of social networks and the Royal Court of Opinion. At any rate, I read it. No anti-humanism and no conversion of anti-humanism into its opposite could have deterred me from absorbing the beauty of these tales of great men, of giving oneself, of chivalry, of Dulcinea. And a part of me saw in this knight errant, in his Sorrowful Countenance, and in his poetic awkwardness, an amazing character who, with a target pinned to his back, struck me as a Christ without apostles whose La Mancha was Galilee, whose Barcelona was another Jerusalem. Or, better, as a righter of wrongs, a valiant knight, a masked avenger ahead of his time, who, after interviewing the Black Mountain convicts one by one, then freeing them, then seeing them turn and betray him, had this to say in reply (a reply that I could have taken as my motto on several occasions in Libya and elsewhere): "Doing good for the bad is like writing in the sand." Only Flaubert knew how to express so forcefully the superiority of lost causes and imaginary battles. Even today, rereading Don Quixote's wonderfully fanciful adventures has evoked in me just one urge: to say to both judges and judged, all those who hold forth about nothing with windy words, that when it comes to wind, you can never do too much tilting at windmills.

To these testimonials I must add the premonition of a Jewishness that I would not discover until later, after completing *Barbarism with a Human Face,* in the kinship of Emmanuel Levinas teaching me to say "after you," showing me that a man's honor consists of standing squarely before others, and repeating often enough to convince me that the only worthwhile philosophy is one that places ethics over ontology. But I was one of those leftist sympathizers (a group larger than was thought) who never succumbed to the infantile disorder of hate for Israel. I have always appreciated the affinity between the universalism to which we aspired as students and the other universalism that, through its will to repair the world and to accompany it on the paths to redemption, constitutes the genius of Judaism. And conversely, when I made my second and true return to Jewishness, which led me to write *The Genius of Judaism,* it is entirely logical that I made Jonah the main character of my odyssey. Of all the prophets, it was he who, in traveling to Nineveh and taking the risk of saving criminals and budding criminals, in urging repentance on people whose descendants, it is written, would spearhead the global war against his people, and in not concerning himself with the absence of evidence that the Ninevites were sincerely repentant even after they began to fast, dress in sackcloth, and beat their breasts, most resembles the committed intellectual that I still am, having spent my life traveling from Dhaka to Misrata, with stops in Luanda, Addis Ababa, and Gaza—that is, from Nineveh to Nineveh.

* * *

That is how a man is made.

How he crystallizes.

And that is how, from such ingredients, the subtle architecture that generates first a reflex and then a commitment is formed.

I have spent time—in the frozen slush of Ukrainian trenches, in the burning savanna of Nigeria, amid the ruins of Mogadishu—breaking bread and sharing daily life with fighting men and women a third my age.

For weeks at a time I have endured fatigue, boredom, and the fear of mines, snipers, and booby-trapped blockhouses to observe disparate people of nearly identical fates; I have recorded tough situations that had settled into stalemate; and occasionally, like Simón Bolívar or Don Quixote, I have plowed the sea.

I have taken risks—and exposed my team to risks—to return after an absence of ten years to western Libya, where I was no longer welcome; to defy Erdoğan under the nose of his mercenaries encamped outside Rojava, knowing that he had me on his hit list; to go fishing for faces in a Somalia where travel had been rare since the 1993 defeat of the Americans at the hands of the Islamist cousins of al-Qaeda, the al-Shabaab, and since the images immortalized in Ridley Scott's *Black Hawk Down* of the bloodied soldiers dragged in the dust behind pickups.

I have spent a great deal of time, truly, fighting against myself, stepping outside my Sartrean comfort zone, and sometimes testing the limits of my strength to put myself in a better position to listen to victims of unadulterated crime and attempt to penetrate its mysteries.

On these adventures, I have left behind a share of my energy and health.

I have devoted resources that others – as Byron said in his last letter to John Bowring, secretary of the London Philhellenic Committee, just before his departure for the Greek isles and Missolonghi, where he died – would have squandered at Almack (a stylish London club open to women as well as men), Newmarket (the equivalent of present-day online horse racing and betting), or other sinkholes of personal pleasure.

No matter how I look at this, the result is the same.

I would not have done what I have if I hadn't had burning within me the feeling, the point of light, the intimate and transcendental conscience, the *reflex* whose genealogy I have just traced.

I would not have had this unusual life – me, comfortable, liberal, born with the privileges for which critics often fault me – if I had not seen before me, in my inner theater, the scene where Fanon's wretched of the earth join Foucault's infamous men, Primo Levi's gaunt ghosts, and (why not?) the battered bodies of Pasolini and the heroic, vanquished athletes of Musset's *Confession of a Child of the Century* in a dance of death – protruding bones against protruding bones, tortured bodies against tortured bodies. That is, if I had not seen it with a dollop of hope, a yearning for fraternity, and a faith in the capacity of man, if not to change the world, at least to prevent it from coming undone, all arising from this ancient inner alchemy.

2

MAN IS NOT A LOCAL ADVENTURE

Fair enough, one might say.

But isn't the struggle against egotism also going on in your own backyard?

And aren't there enough poor people in Europe, or in America, to spare you the trouble of looking for more in the tents of the Moria refugee camp or the slums of Bangladesh?

Since how I spend my time is not really the issue, I am not going to justify myself against this charge or present evidence of service closer to home.

But here is another confession I have never made in quite this way or in these terms, one that will respond, I hope, to critics of good faith.

One of the notions of my youth to which I remain obscurely faithful, despite its history, its sinister cargo, and the distance I've traveled since I encountered it for the first time, is internationalism. Internationalism is getting bad press today.

* * *

I do not mean globalism.

And I wish to make clear that I have never had any special sympathy for the generalized, unchained capitalism that is implied by globalization of trade and production.

No fascination with its mechanisms.

Hardly any curiosity about the human adventures, the success stories, of its heroes: Bezos, Soros, Zuckerberg, and so on.

In fact, I am rather embarrassed—thanks to my youthful leftism—by the economistic obsession that a world enchanted by globalization imposes on us.

The same goes for Europe!

When Europe's leaders present us with a free-trade zone capable of nurturing global champions of manufacturing and finance, my interest perks up—but no more than that.

When I write *Hôtel Europe* and then adapt it for a European tour, I say, yes, of course, to building out the European system as designed by Konrad Adenauer and Jean Monnet, which, following the nationalist horror, was the lifeline of our parents' generation. But my yes is an anxious and unenthusiastic one, based solely on the negative premise that you can't do anything with nothing—and certainly not with the reaction, hate, and resentment of Europhobes like Jean-Luc Mélenchon and Marine Le Pen or Steve Bannon. As for this soulless Union, in thrall to the worst of domination-by-spectacle, this Europe of identical streets, cookie-cutter malls, and business districts speaking the same global English and haunted by the same despair—yesterday superconsumerist, today burrowed into locked-down molehills—well, you have to have read me wrong to believe that I celebrate that and, further, to know very little about me not to comprehend that the only Europe I venerate is the one beloved of

Stefan Zweig and Romain Rolland; the one Goethe had in mind when he remarked to Johann Peter Eckermann that no one in Europe seemed as great to him as Molière, one of whose plays he made a point of rereading each year; the Europe of the Viennese cafés where Beethoven burst out in anger as he watched Napoleon, to whom he had dedicated his Eroica symphony, transform himself into a tyrant—which is to say, an ordinary man trampling the rights of man after the composer had, like his near-twin, Hegel, mistaken him for the soul of the world and of revolution.

Many, many times have I written, uttered, shouted that my Europe, the only one that commands my passion and my time, is the one where, as one walks the streets strewn with fast-food signs and shops selling junk made in Bangladeshi sweatshops, one somehow manages still to encounter the ghosts of Kafka, Canetti, Pessoa, and Joyce, of Eduard Mörike describing Mozart directing, in Prague, the first performances of *Don Juan*.

And I trust I needn't dot the i's when I say that institutional Europe, the Europe of regulated appliances, holds my respect chiefly because of the continent's terrible past, which will have to get around today's institutional Europe before it can raise its ugly head again.

* * *

Nor do I mean cosmopolitanism.

I have used the word, of course.

I have enjoyed turning into a source of pride a term that, not so long ago, was used to heap opprobrium on people like me.

And I once delivered an apologia on behalf of a cosmopolitan spirit that seemed to me the proper path to freedom, against "the France of backyards, berets, binges, and Breton bagpipes."

But although I do not disown that, and although I still find chauvinism as odious as I did thirty years ago, I have come to believe that there is something in the word that is not quite right.

What bothers me, with the passage of time, is the "polis" in cosmopolite.

Of course, the term continues to evoke in me, as it does in everyone, the great Greek cities that were one of the sources, in the West, of the modern democratic invention. But what troubles me is its resonance with what I am suddenly tempted to call "ancient Greek ideology," borrowing from my *Idéologie Française* of forty years ago.

By this I mean a triple trap that language remembers even when we who speak it may have forgotten it.

First, there are the distinctions among the various ways of inhabiting that polis: citizens, metics, freed slaves now owning slaves of their own, half- or quarter-slaves possessing the right to be employed as sailors, and so on. I knew all that by heart during my Hellenizing youth. It, too, was part of the Greek polis – a diabolically complex social architecture in no way outdone by the brutality of the Indian caste system.

Next there is the fact that each polis has its cults, its priests, and its temples, which remain, in law and in fact, closed to inhabitants of other polises. The great nineteenth-century historian Fustel de Coulanges, author of *The Ancient City* (1864), recounts that Athenians were forbidden to enter the temple of Hera in Argos, just as the people of Argos were denied entry to the equivalent temple in Athens. And since the lares, penates, genies, demons, and heroes peculiar to each city were other names for the souls of citizens "made divine by death," it follows that foreigners – that is, people from another polis – were treated not as residents of another political entity where they enjoyed similar rights, but as barbarians.

And finally, what about the third type of "other" in this ancient paradigm, one who is neither a domestic other (metic, slave) nor a foreign other (barbarian, enemy), but rather the other of the borderlands? What was the status of those from the outlying regions of the Greek polis or the Roman city, areas that we would now call outlying suburbs? And what are we to make of a form of citizenship that, according to Fustel de Coulanges on the birth of Rome, ends at the furrows formed by the legendary founder's plow? The historian can say all he wants that Romulus was a "leader of adventurers." He can insist that Romulus "created a people by summoning vagabonds and thieves." The fact is that soon enough there was intra muros Rome, built on Palatine Hill and reserved for former residents of Alba Longa, themselves heirs to the noble lineage of Aeneas, and that "the people," composed of vagabonds and thieves, were immediately banished to Capitoline Hill, the first site of exile in Western history. So can we say that Athens and early Rome are models of great republics? Archetypes of the modern city in Europe or America? For someone who travels the globe to promote principled policies toward exiled persons and who, when he returns, proclaims the need to rethink laws and regulations on the treatment of migrants, the ancient city of Plato and Aristotle, but also of Dionysus of Halicarnassus and Dion Cassius, is another source of mistrust.

* * *

I say mistrust.

Not loathing.

Because internationalism, to my mind – and here's where things get complicated—is not synonymous with the rejection of localized cities or the national model of the modern era.

Make no mistake, I have nothing but disdain for chauvinistic ravings.

And, like Thomas Bernhard and others, I maintain that patriotism is sometimes the lout's version of virtue.

But the strangest thing about the adventure whose most recent episodes are reported in this book but whose history runs through my entire life is that it is not unaccompanied, under certain circumstances, by a pride that Bernhard called (making fun of himself) "the country of the fathers."

I possess none of the honors bestowed by academia or science. I have never sought nor received from my country any sort of medal or prize. I have made it a matter of principle never to assume any official function. But, that said, I have on several occasions placed my international activism in the service of the French Republic.

During the Bosnian war there were the two coups that I recounted in *Le Lys et la Cendre,* my journal of the time. Having managed to exfiltrate Bosnia's president, Alija Izetbegović, from the hell of his besieged capital and bring him to Paris, I was able to arrange a hasty audience for him with President François Mitterrand, who had earlier invited himself to Sarajevo.

A few years later, after the fall of the Taliban and the death of Commander Massoud—whom I had earlier tried, this time in vain, to bring to see President Jacques Chirac—I spent long months squatting in an empty, abandoned, bombarded French embassy in Kabul, as Chirac's special envoy. Far from the metropole—but still France!

There are the eight Kurdish commanders, led by General Sirwan Barzani, whom I met in the trenches facing the ISIS lines and was able to escort, in their Peshmerga uniforms, through the corridors of the Élysée Palace during the presidency of François Hollande.

There is the strange position in which I found myself the following year in Ukraine, when I agreed to represent France alongside the presidents of Germany, Ukraine, and Poland for the commemoration of the seventy-fifth anniversary of the massacre of thirty-three thousand Jews buried in the ravines of Babi Yar.

There is the war in Libya, of course, for which I have been lavishly criticized.

And, on the sidelines of one of the pieces of reporting collected here, there is the satisfaction of having served as a messenger for President Emmanuel Macron to honor Bangladesh's half century of independence.

And, in another of these pieces, there is a memorable telephone conversation where the same President Macron announced his increased support for the leader of the Kurdish army in Rojava, General Mazloum Kobani Abdi, who was hunkered down in his bunker, the target of Ankara's drones.

"The man who whispers in presidents' ears." That is how French journalist Benoît Duquesne described me at the end of an "extended investigation" that purported to tell the story of my life. I did not like that image. It gave off a whiff of conspiracy that is quite unlike me. And I distrust, as Lawrence would say, that "ground-level tomb" occupied by any writer who gives in to a political order. But it did convey a glimmer of truth. And Duquesne's documentary did have the virtue of reporting the strange game that I have sometimes allowed myself to play, one in which I have chosen to serve my country—without ever spending too much time wondering who was using whom and who was being exploited by what.

All the more so because there are more cases, and more distinctive ones, where I am representing no one, where no one has vested in me any power whatsoever, where no one in Paris has been informed of my movements or conferred upon me any mission, where I have no mandate other than the one that—by aberration, presumption, or, to speak again like Stéphane Mallarmé, divagation—I have sovereignly bestowed upon myself. But the moment always arrives when I surprise myself not only by speaking in the name of France but also by feeling real joy when I sense that my divagation is echoed by those to whom it is addressed—or, even better, when the divagation amplifies and reinforces the effect of my action.

That day in Benghazi's Tahrir Square at the height of the Libyan revolution when I addressed a crowd of Arabs waving flags of several nations, including France.

The same scene in Maidan Square in Kiev where, several days before, the crowd had been subjected to live fire only to return in greater numbers to listen to greetings from a French writer addressing them in French.

The same scene fifteen years earlier, in Heroes' Square in Vienna, which Thomas Bernhard had made the title of his last play and where I spoke to two hundred thousand young people as a far-right government was coming to power, assuring them of the solidarity of a Frenchman who believed that tolerance of fascism died in the death camps.

And still others, so many other scenes, where the same motif recurred and I found myself—Jew, metic, an atheist to all—presenting my country's greetings to crowds bowled over by the unexpected support.

The man who takes himself, not for Napoleon, but for an envoy of France . . .

The perpetual self-proclaimed plenipotentiary of a France that had not summoned me and to which I have never failed to speak the truth as I saw it, no matter how unpleasant . . .

And, in accounts designed above all else to give voice to the voiceless and to shed a narrow shaft of light on a forgotten war or unseen misery, I always sought a way to address my own nation, a France rich in glory and laden with infamy, full of grace but also having done wrong—as if I were pressing it to speak, to say out loud whether it was still up to the challenges of history; whether its tongue, its fluent tongue, the language of Descartes and Voltaire, Sartre and Malraux, were doomed to provincialism, or whether it might yet be a language of politics.

That sounds absurd.

Even I have to smile at it.

But that's how it is.

I love France.

I love the fact that it has been great.

I love that it can still be great.

And if—through one of the initiatives that set the diplomats aflutter (and, with a few exceptions, make them detest me)—I can make that greatness ring, that is enough for me.

* * *

I emphasize France.

When I set out for distant lands to plead for *liberté*, *égalité*, and *fraternité*, two great scenes are always present to my mind – two that, in my view, define the standard of French greatness: Free France and France's participation in the adventure of the international brigades in Spain.

As I've said, both resound in my family history.

Both are synonymous with courage and therefore contain the highest possible share of nobility of anything found in this world.

Both also share the merit of having attracted simple, ordinary people: lost children of the Republic, up from nowhere; unfortunates, as the poet François Villon said, lacking privilege, place, or face; half-breeds, as General de Gaulle said half a millennium later in London's Olympia Hall; Moroccan soldiers under French colonial command; Jews, so many Jews, coming to Spain in December 1937 to join the second company of the Palafox battalion of the international brigades, who would resurface later, after a spell in the French camps at Gur and Saint-Cyprien, in Resistance units made up of immigrant volunteers (FTP-MOI).

But I realize that if I had to choose between the two, if, God forbid, I had to favor one and only one of these two fraternities, my reasoning would be as follows: despite everything I know about its dark side, despite the Soviet gangrene that ate away at it, despite the Comintern's liquidation of the POUMists, despite the accounts of George Orwell, Arthur Koestler, and John Dos Passos, despite André Malraux's response to Victor Serge when the latter raised the matter of the POUM ("I accept Stalin's crimes"), and despite Victor Serge then flinging the contents of his cup in Malraux's face – despite all that, I would choose the Spanish fraternity.

For three reasons.

First, I wonder whether the historians who have studied that dark side may not have overstated their case.

After the Molotov-Ribbentrop Pact, didn't Stalin disown the brigades, caught as he was in the maze of his own machinations and deeming that the glory, the glow, but also the unpredictability of these old-timers had rendered them inconvenient?

Isn't it true that they saw their commanders purged in turn by agents of a KGB that suddenly wanted no more "paper artillery" or "sublime epics," the fancy names of the propaganda operations carried out by the Comintern?

And what of the case of André Marty, the "inspector general" of the brigades, who was allegedly responsible for ordering five hundred deaths by firing squad? That conclusion is not confirmed by the contemporary testimony of Henri Rol-Tanguy, not by the intervening work of Jacques Delperrié de Bayac, and not by the more recent work of Rémi Skoutelsky. Is Marty's case as clear-cut as some have made it out to be? Did the model for André Massart in *For Whom the Bell Tolls* really deserve the awful name of "butcher of Albacete"?

That aside, I love the mythology this theme has attracted, before and after its expression in Spain.

Are people aware that the inventor of the model, a full century earlier, is none other than a certain Lord Byron, who was haunted by the failed attempt of the veterans of the Napoleonic Wars to rally to the support of Simón Bolívar and urged the London Philhellenic Committee to absorb the lessons of their effort and apply them to the Greeks' struggle against the Ottoman Empire?

And are they aware that André Malraux, haunted by Byron's

example and cognizant of having fulfilled it by forming and commanding the España air squadron, spent the rest of his life trying to repeat the exploit? There was the plan for an international brigade for Chile in 1949, with Paul Nothomb; a roughly similar plan at the time of the Suez crisis and the threat it posed to the existence of the young state of Israel; and, of course, the international brigade for Bangladesh that he launched in the twilight of his life as one last leap of faith from his admirable youth, which made so much difference at the dawn of mine.

But what most entrances me in the history of these brigades is perhaps the word *international.* If I am inclined toward them, if no historical criticism has succeeded in dampening my esteem for them, that is because they, more than any others, exhibit the quality of bringing together people of all sorts from all sorts of places, the capacity that nations sometimes have, mine in particular, to speak more than their own language.

Free France was a shadow army.

It was the English radio broadcasts that listeners from Paris to Lyon, including the maquis cells of the Auvergne, tuned into clandestinely and avidly.

It was the beauty of the flight to London, where Jews and the aristocrats of the nativist Action Française would come to know each other and work together for the rebirth of France.

But it was only France.

It was magnificent; it was heroic; but it centered on the liberation of a single country, transcended by the struggle against the evil of Nazism.

Whereas, with the brigades, the scale was the world.

They were composed of cohorts of dreamers and amateurs gathered from all over the planet.

They were the Czechoslovakians Lise and Artur London crossing paths with the Duchess of Atholl, the eccentric Nancy Cunard, and the unpredictable Upton Sinclair.

They were the Americans of the Abraham Lincoln Brigade, its ranks filled out with Cypriots, Chileans, Mexicans, and, according to Alejo Carpentier, several hundred Cubans.

There was the Ukrainian Ilya Ehrenburg, officially a correspondent for *Izvestia* (and even, some will say, the greatest reporter of the twentieth century), portrayed by Hemingway as a red condottiere waging war "for his own account."

There were the Serbian and Croatian units.

Dutch volunteers.

Slaves.

There was Dombrowski's Polish brigade, which comprised as many Belorussians as Poles.

There was the Garibaldi brigade, which went into combat alongside Ernst Thälmann's hundred.

The February 12 Battalion, which, though its name does not suggest it, was composed of Austrians.

The New Nations Battalion, which, as its name suggests, consisted of volunteers from nine nations.

There was the Naftali Botwin Brigade, with its 135 Jewish riflemen, whom the enemy called red devils and who received their orders in four languages.

And for France, there were the volunteers of the Liberty Column commanded by Italian anti-fascists; the Paris Commune Hundred, in which Walloons equipped with Remingtons also served; the Franco-Belgian Louise Michel Battalion; English novelist Ralph Fox and poet Rupert John Cornford as members of the Marseillaise Battalion; the barefoot Ukrainians of the Taras Shevchenko Company who had been fitted out with shoes, jerseys, and overalls in Toulouse; there was Henri Cartier-Bresson filming the young Yankees of the Abraham Lincoln Brigade; and there were the five hundred Algerians who for nothing in the world would let it be said that the "Moors" were all on the side of the Francoists and who – like Mohamed Belaïdi, machine gunner in the André Malraux air squadron, killed in the sky over Teruel and depicted in *Man's Fate* in a casket covered with a Muslim crescent – fought alongside Parisian volunteers.

The international brigades were all that.

They were the bohemians and stateless wanderers that Largo Caballero was never able to completely incorporate into the regular Spanish army.

They were Noah's Ark, an unreconstructed Tower of Babel, a polyglot boardinghouse.

The international brigades were the human race.

And it is because their members were not fighting for themselves, for France, or even for Spain that I see them – that we have always seen them, and here I am speaking for myself as well as Marc Roussel and Gilles Hertzog, my two most frequent team members – as an epitome of greatness and brotherhood.

* * *

I would like to say a little about Gilles Hertzog.

Although reporting is often a group adventure; although I am indebted to Marc Roussel and, further back, Alexis Duclos, for their photographic work; although my documentary films stand or fall on the images of intrepid cameramen (Camille Lotteau, Olivier Jacquin, Ala Tayyeb) and even a producer (François Margolin) who traveled into the field with us for three of the films, unheard of for someone in his position, no one has supported me for as long as Gilles. My other great friend, Jean-Paul Enthoven, introduced us nearly fifty years ago: it was toward the end of 1974. I had just returned from Bangladesh; he was coming out of an unhappy love affair. And we, along with Michel Butel, set out to launch a daily newspaper, *L'Imprévu*. Since then no one has been so closely involved in so many of my life's adventures – indeed, nearly all of them. So, at this point, and though his name may be unfamiliar to most of my French readers (and, I daresay, to even more of my American audience), I feel I need to tell the reader who he is and say how much I owe to him.

As the grandson of Marcel Cachin, the founder of the French Communist Party, Gilles experienced even more intimately than I the pains of the break with communist tradition, with communism's crimes, and with its dreams.

And because his parents were among those who, on behalf of the party, founded France Navigation, the shipping company responsible for transporting "arms for Spain" from Baltic ports to Bilbao and Bordeaux, he, like me, grew up worshipping what he called, in the book he coauthored in 1984 with philosopher Dominique-Antoine Grisoni, the "sea brigades."

Which is to say that he was wellborn.

Please understand that, from my lips, being wellborn does not mean being pulled out of Jupiter's thigh, like Dionysus.

Or being born with a silver spoon in his mouth.

It means: exposed from birth to the tempests of the time.

It means: taken over, early on, by obsessive fear of the all-consuming absolutes of grand policy.

And it means: informed – though at a high cost, though only by having absorbed the torpedoes of the family dogmatism and the missiles of family members who were among the last real Stalinists in France, though only by having suffered the blows from the hammers and sickles of two radical parents who, when we met, had demanded that he choose between the "New Philosophy" and the Party – informed, therefore, that history is a fact, that it is tragic, and that, all too often, it is a dead end.

Otherwise, Gilles is one of the most romantic characters I know.

A real presence with a loud voice and a laugh that, if anything, is too deep.

Up for anything.

A soft heart under the brashness.

Capable of dying from love and consenting to get well only if it meant taking off for Ethiopia or Rwanda.

A taste for greatness, boldness.

In one of my documentaries he can be seen shaking his handsome head, tired from several takes, while I compose an appeal to the international community that I intend to have signed by a Libyan leader. He loses his patience only after I, having already put in the Libyan's mouth an allusion to Free France, balk at capitalizing the "free" in the phrase.

And the white mane that was often, in circumstances that I will someday describe in detail, another form of his panache.

Writing little but speaking volumes, he is credited with some extraordinary remarks.

Like this one from the time of the Bosnian war, uttered in the Sorbonne's grand amphitheater, as full as it ever was in its best days, flung in the face of Alain Juppé, then minister of foreign affairs, whom I had invited to an academic discussion of Europe and culture: "Mr. Minister of National Resignation, Bosnia's dead salute you!" It was like a Bickford fuse that set off a wave of jeering that we hadn't seen there since the turmoil of May 1968. The minister, drained of color, had to gather up his things under a hail of hurrahs and projectiles. And because he didn't know my Gilles and was unaware that he cannot be restrained when he believes that something essential is at stake, Juppé, to this day, believes I set a trap for him by extending him a polite invitation only to have him humiliated by unrestrained Bosnians and Rwandans.

Or that Christmas Eve when we decided on the spur of the moment—and with no time to prepare those close to us—to make yet another visit to Bosnia. "And your family, your children?" his wife, an Italian duchess, asked him when he phoned her from a booth at the airport. "Did you think about your family's Christmas? Your children's?" To which he, pressured because the flight was boarding, pushed to the limits, and perhaps no longer seeing clearly, responded: "Between Bosnia and the family, today I choose Bosnia." Her terse reply: "If that's the way it is, I divorce you!" Which she did upon his return, plunging him into one of those bouts of lovesickness to which he was so prone and causing him later to set out to become, for the purpose of winning her over, a true expert in Italian and Venetian painting.

In reacting as she did, she may well have had other reasons of which I am unaware.

What I am sure of, however, is that *his* statement, his inversion of Camus's formula – "Between justice and my mother, I choose my mother" – will seem shocking only to those blinded by family romance novels. It had something of the bravado of chivalrous knights consumed by avoiding choices between their fair lady and their duty. It is also an example of what we used to call commitment or, in the language of philosophers viewed askance by the likes of the Hertzogs and Cachins, *responsibility for others.*

For no one lives more in the present than he does, and no one has as much sense of and affection for the beautiful past.

He does not watch television, but he has Chateaubriand at his fingertips.

He confuses Google with Wikipedia, does not know how to use the Internet, but has all the answers on the historic rivalry between the Turkish and Russian Empires.

Only one thing can distract him from our campaigns: his love of painting, and not just Italian painting. He inherited that love from a family that included one Impressionist and supported several others. It is a pretty good antidote to his more rigid postures.

I said that he was born without a silver spoon.

That's not entirely accurate.

His father, who was married to the redoubtable Marcelle Cachin, a member of the National Assembly, was official surgeon to those whom the post-Stalin *nomenklatura* considered very important patients, such as walking-dead rulers clinging to their power. Nevertheless, or perhaps as a result, he was quite rich.

But Gilles incurred ruin a first time by loving a woman who

"was not in [his] style," as Swann said of Odette. Faithful to a long-held and ineradicable principle that caused him to place on the same footing what Balzac would have called courtesans and princesses, he let her fleece him thoroughly.

And then a second and final time because he had refused to inform financial regulators about the activities of a woman whom he did not love but who was the wife of one of our friends: he could not bear to see her "accused without proof"; now, this veritable Bernie Madoff in heels was in the process of burning through the proceeds of sales of the Pissarros, the Signacs, and the private clinics that his cold-hearted parents had unintentionally bequeathed to him – "I didn't like that money," he told me when the Madoff was unmasked, "or any money, for that matter – we live well enough on the riches of time . . . "

The difference between an aristocrat and a bourgeois is well known, even if today it is often forgotten. It lies not in a title but in a word: disinterestedness.

A man capable of being rich one day and broke the next without provoking any change in him – in his elegance, freedom, or vitality – that is a disinterested man.

A man who will place his peace of mind and his career after a cause for which he is ready to fight to his physical limits (the cause of Sarajevo's children, of the villagers of Darfur hunted down by Khartoum's cavalry, of Nigeria's Christians, or of Kurdish women whose combat uniforms cannot conceal their hope for a real life in a real home) – that is a champion.

A man capable of daydreaming endlessly before a Tiepolo or a Titian (and of passing on his passion to his son) and who, from one day to the next – *because it's necessary* – takes off trekking across the desert in broken-down, stinking jeeps, surrounded by rough-and-tough fighters totally unaware of his cultivated nature and other fine points – that is a chivalrous man.

Such is Gilles.

Both big brother and little brother.

Miraculous repository of my doubts, my secrets, and my expectations, which always find in him an open ear and a closed mouth.

The man who, on the eve of our last trip to Libya – frustrated at not being able to persuade me that we were walking (he said he could sense it) into danger more serious than usual and which, in fact, took the form of an ambush – wound up saying, "I'd walk with you into hell, but this time, let me tell you, it will be worthy of Dante." Despite which, because he is my friend and is one of the few who puts friendship high on the scale of values and passions, he did indeed walk in.

"Everything is shared between friends," Hölderlin said, citing Aristotle.

Well, not everything, of course.

In any case, not the limelight that he leaves to me with incomparable generosity whenever we return from our journeys.

Often in literary friendships the greater celebrity that one or the other receives alters the quality of the friendship. In his case, celebrity figures not at all in the mutual bond that we share and exercise, equally, in the secrecy of our ordeals and the darkness of our quest.

I pity anyone who has not experienced the heavenly gift of a true friend, an eternal friend, a friend as transparent as water from a rocky stream. A friend.

* * *

Now, to sum up . . .

When I say *internationalism,* I am thinking of the world, but with the proviso that it should no longer be a standardized wasteland where, as Pasolini said, "the farther you go, the less different it is."

I am thinking of cosmopolitanism, but on the condition of including in the cosmos those exiled from the polis, its foreigners and outcasts, the uncounted, the untouchable, the unheard, those living beyond the holy wall of the city and – because these have supplanted the city – the wall of the nation and the state. Or, as the Greeks would have put it, those excluded from the distribution of meat following sacrifices. Or those not entitled to own land or to participate in the democratic life of the agora or the palaestra. Or the agents of a great replacement, already feared in ancient Athens, who would usurp the places of electors. (Plutarch tells us that Pericles, ordinarily so predisposed to foreigners, ordered that five thousand metics found guilty of having passed themselves off as citizens be sold into slavery.) Yes, I would keep the word but only after making it sing with the voices of the excluded, those we now refer to, in today's democracies, as migrants, immigrants, foreigners without and foreigners within. And if I keep it, it is in the knowledge that the ranks of the world's excluded are larger still: crowds without parish, Panathenaea, or panegyrics of any kind; multitudes of men, women, and children for whom life promises so very little, who are not and never will be archons, strategists, or even metics for the simple reason that they inhabit badlands where there is no polis at all.

Turning now to the Internationale – of which I sometimes have the feeling of being one of the last members, along with reporters and the expatriates of the NGOs – it has never bothered me when the Internationale issues its commandments from a particular nation, or even in that nation's name and for that nation's greater glory – provided the nation in question is, like America or Israel, an idea as well as a piece of ground; that the nation strives, like all ideas, to dialogue with other ideas of the same sort; that a European, for example, should feel compelled, to paraphrase Bernhard again, to think in French when he is speaking German or in German when speaking French; that it invokes an expanding Universal rather than a local genius brined in identity; and that, as a consequence, it has the capacity to be greater than itself, to be great for a great number of people, and to speak to the rest of the human race (even beyond the extent permitted by the physics of small and midsize powers).

I'm not saying the task is an easy one.

The desire to speak not to France alone, not to Europe alone, not to the United States alone, but to the world; the concern for justice, ideally applied not just to a given city that is ignoring its metics within and without, but to all cities, as well as to that part of the world where people do not know what a city of citizens even means; the wish to be able to feel at home anywhere, even where tyrants are triumphant or the spirit of Nineveh reigns – none of that, I am well aware, comes easily.

Indeed, it was the stumbling block of early Christianity with its idea of a universal church in which people would no longer be Jews or Greeks; and then of the German and French Enlightenment, with its notions of a cosmopolitan law applicable irrespective of time, place, or circumstance; and earlier, of that obscure corner of Greek thought, unjustly disdained, that gave expression to the dream of Diogenes of Sinope and the Cynics of a man who felt close enough to other men that he could be a "beggar, vagabond, living day to day, without city, without home, without country."

Just as there is, according to Emmanuel Levinas, easy freedom and difficult freedom, so perhaps there are easy and difficult forms of the fight against egotism – and of the fight *for* justice.

The easy form? The one that begins and ends at my own door, in my relations with people who resemble me and of whom I have some personal experience. The one that, for Hegel (citing Goethe), pokes fun at the man who "plays the great man" to the outside world and regards himself as "a living miracle," but who is called to order by "his wife and his valet." Acting on the universal stage is an illusion! It is in private, close to one's own, that a man is himself and reveals his greatness! Faraway strangers are not his business! The one that, translated into contemporary political language, comes to manifest itself in the rancid idea known right and left as sovereignism – or in the purportedly commonsensical saying of Jean-Marie Le Pen, that consummate political street performer of the last century: "I prefer my daughter to my cousin, my cousin to my neighbor, my neighbor to my countrymen, and my countrymen to Europeans!"

The difficult form? The one that can spot the baseness at work in the celebrated sentence just quoted, contrasting it term by term with Montesquieu's courageous wisdom: "If I knew something that was useful to me and prejudicial to my family, I would put it out of my mind; if I knew something that was useful to my family but not to my country, I would try to forget it; if I knew something that was useful to country and prejudicial to Europe and the human race, I would regard it as a crime." The form that – having bound me to Europe because it is greater than France, to the world because it is greater than Europe, and to anyplace where I can detect not necessarily the spirit but evidence of it—links me to men and women about whom I may have only a vague and sometimes abstract idea, but to whom I am drawn as if they were as close as brothers; the form that maintains that solidarity has no limit, that justice is no different on one side of a border than on the other, and that it is no crazier to sympathize with the words of a Bangladeshi, the call for justice of an unveiled Iranian woman, the rights of an archaic Tibetan, or those of a horseman imagined by Joseph Kessel, even if I have no personal perception of any of them, than with the troubles of a Parisian kid from a bad neighborhood or the challenges of a laid-off worker whose benefits are running out and whose life seems to have been brusquely yanked away.

If I defend the difficult form; if, instead of staying home as recommended by the Great Fear that was settling in as I made the first of this new series of reports, I moved toward places where people who have no home in which to wait out the pandemic were living and dying; if, when I was being exhorted to isolate as a form of commitment, to retrench as a form of solidarity, and, in short, to confine myself—if, under those circumstances, I persisted in traveling to Lesbos and Jessore, to stateless Kurds cast adrift by nations that deny them the right to be our brothers, to cursed Mogadishu, to abandoned Donbass, to crumbling Afghanistan, it was probably out of defiance.

But it was also *because* it seemed relatively "easy," yes, to hunker down at home, rather than to commune with faraway people, to sketch faces that are not like ours, to see them in their diversity and multiplicity, that I made the choice I did. In *Le Démon de l'Absolu,* Malraux lauds T. E. Lawrence's exceptional memory, which retained, even after the passage of years, precise recollections of places, landscapes, and the sun sparkling on the snows of Edom. But even that exceptional memory is not enough: Malraux deplored the poverty of the portraits in *The Seven Pillars.* Characters without depth, reduced to soulless stereotypes! And the painful impression the book gives of "a sandstorm managed by ghosts more starlike than human!"

And even if "easy" doesn't work, it seems clear enough that although some people concern themselves with the victims of injustice in the West (bravo!), very few travel to the other side of the world, into lands of banishment such as Somalia and Bangladesh. I say yes to compassion and openness for those crossing the Rio Grande in search of a better life. And I say no to the detention centers of the previous American president. But the disgust and anger behind that "yes" and that "no" also apply to the migrant souls waiting hopelessly at the gates of Europe in Moria. I say yes to women's liberation in the West, but just as much indignation and solidarity are due with respect to the women of Afghanistan, who fear losing their hard-earned rights if, with the confirmed American withdrawal, the Taliban regains control. And isn't it good economics, then—just pure, simple good economics—that men and women who care about the public good divide up the task and decide not to all work in the same way, with the same tools, and in the same places?

Kudos, surely, to the organizations like David Miliband's International Rescue Committee in Moria, and others in Lampedusa, Calais, Roscoff, and Queens that hold out a hand to those excluded from Panathenaea and the distribution of meats.

A shout-out to the humanitarians who, while I was pursuing my task, devoted themselves to rescuing the new poor produced by the lockdown of economies after the outbreak of the pandemic.

And, by the way, with the same team that accompanied me to Nigeria and Syria, I spent several weekends reporting on the distribution of hot meals in Paris's Place de la République, reports that appeared in my weekly column in *Le Point.*

But if one has the desire, the energy, and the means, both logistical and media-related, why not try to do both?

In places where humanitarian organizations are few or nonexistent, why not try to be present?

And what kind of Europe would it be if there were no more young people to push to the limits the realm of brotherhood, human rights, and law?

In the cities of democratic states, I see the rise of injustice—and of incivility, cruelty, racism, and anti-Semitism.

But among those whom Fanon dubbed the wretched of the earth, I see an explosion of extreme misery; even more marked inequality in the face of the virus and the devastating effects of climate change; I observe that the most unjust of injustices, the mother of all the others, is more than ever one's luck in being born in one latitude rather than another, in a temperate part of the planet rather than in its accursed zones, not to mention those whom *no* nation recognizes as rightful citizens, those of whom no one wants to know where they were born or where they will die, and who, by virtue of a paradox stripped of its mystery by Hannah Arendt and Giorgio Agamben, are deprived of human rights precisely because they are *no more* than human.

That is a great menace.

Never in the modern age—that is, since the world globalized—has humanity been so separated from itself, so divided.

And never has the unity of the human race, a fragile but sacred principle since the origins of the Judeo-Christian West, been so monstrously challenged.

My internationalism is a response to that.

I don't know if *internationalism* is even the right word, but I don't have a better one to describe the necessary resistance to the storm gathering at civilization's core.

And this series of reports, which began as a commission from a major magazine but continued through hell and high water, through a pandemic against which the world locked itself down and turned within, also served the purpose of reaffirming the simple but imperiled idea that man is not a local adventure; that a person is as much all people as he is an individual person; and that therein lies the greatness of humanism, which it falls to us to reinvent a half century after Michel Foucault and his anthologies of brief lives, misfortunes without number, and misfortunates deemed unworthy of attention.

I can say it in the language of Mozart: I am a writer who, confronted with the danger in humanity's house, and unlike Alexander dreaming (according to *Don Giovanni*) whether there were other worlds he might try to conquer, remembers that there is but one world, one, over which the empire of human rights must come to extend.

I can say it as a Jew who, like Haim de Volozhin, the great Lithuanian rabbi of the late eighteenth and early nineteenth century, writing in *The Soul of Life,* sees the coming apart, sees Creation being uncreated (and desecrated) in a sort of reverse Big Bang that blasts masses of surplus people into nothingness, and who assigns himself the task of doing what it is in his power to do (prayer and study, words and "reporting") to keep the roof beams that allow the human race to live, if not under one roof, then at least under one sky, from collapsing.

And finally, I can say it as a writer who dreams of a place (never mind if real or imagined) where Kessel's horsemen could dialogue with Malaparte's, the *Anatolian Village* of Mahmut Makal with Faulkner's *Hamlet* and his *Mansion,* the characters of Rabindranath Tagore (whom I discovered a half-century ago in Bangladesh) with those of Shelley or Shakespeare's *Hamlet,* Wole Soyinka's King Baabu with Alfred Jarry's Ubu, Strabo's Orpheus with Philip Glass's *Orphée,* the young women of Jane Austen with Dostoyevsky's possessed or Mishima's suicides. Are they not all facets of one humanity, one that true thought, true generosity, and a true metaphysics cannot possibly conceive as separate?

3

INTO THE UNKNOWN

But that's not all.

And because I resolved to be sincere, to pull off the masks, and not to dress myself up in grand principles and lofty sentiments, I must not lie about, conceal, or deny what liberated me.

There was another book that was important to me in my youth.

I could not say whether this one counted for me alone or for my generation.

Nor can I recall with as much precision as for *The Wretched of the Earth* the circumstances in which I discovered it. A first edition from Sagittaire in my mother's library? A later edition from Grasset during the first year of my preparation for the École Normale Supérieure? Later?

What I know for certain is that it was in my pocket like a viaticum at the time of my departure for Bangladesh in 1971.

Another certainty is that, although I did not reread it until now, it hovered in my mind during all the years I spent practicing the profession of reporting.

The book was entitled *Portrait of the Adventurer.*

A mixture of Malraux, Lawrence, and Ernst von Salomon, author of *Les Réprouvés* and one of the assassins of Walter Rathenau, it was a topsy-turvy text containing, "by way of conclusion," a long and bizarre biographical note on the military chief of the Paris Commune, Louis Rossel. No one was sure how it got there. This book, too, had a preface by Sartre.

The man who wrote it, Roger Stéphane, was a strange character, a friend of Cocteau and Gide, less author than dealer or stroller, an unrepentant dandy, openly gay, living large, forever a Gaullist, a hero of Free France, twice imprisoned by the Vichy regime and inconsolable at having missed out on the international brigades.

His name will not mean much to my younger readers.

I came to know him a few years after my return from Bangladesh.

He contacted me and André Glucksmann when our New Philosophy movement was gathering steam.

And I remember lunching with him at his home on the Rue Ernest Psichari, a little apartment done up in a grand manner where we were served by a butler, which was decidedly uncommon in literary circles, and where he spent two hours prodding us, with the delectation of an elder who had been waiting for this moment for thirty years, to talk about our anti-totalitarian itineraries borrowed from the left; about our rapport with Solzhenitsyn; about why, in my *Barbarism with a Human Face,* I described the author of *The Gulag Archipelago* as the "Dante of our time"; about François Mitterrand, whom he detested; about General de Gaulle, whom he worshipped; about the comparative merits, in our view, of the Bernard Pivot show that had just launched us and of one that he himself had produced a few years earlier, during the time of the ORTF (the French national radio and television orchestra).

I saw him several times after that, until his suicide in 1994.

On those occasions, I prodded him on Malraux, Lawrence, his reasons for overlooking von Salomon's anti-Semitism (which was, for me, indisputable), and the Compagnons de la Libération, about whom he wanted to produce a television special.

I admired his fluency, his humor, his aspect of a man of action in a bow tie recounting how he had liberated the Hôtel de Ville as Maurice Clavel did Chartres and Hemingway the Ritz.

I saw him near the end, when – sick, broke, and badgered by his creditors and the French tax authorities – he still would come to Le Récamier, the restaurant in Saint-Germain-des-Prés where publishers indulged their most valuable writers and Martin Cantegrit, the owner, when he wasn't sending one of his waiters to serve Stéphane at home, continued to reserve the best table for him and let him lunch for free.

Anyway, what was in *Portrait of the Adventurer?*

It was not really the apologia of the adventurer that those who have not read it or who, like me, read it a long time ago and were living on its memory, believed it to be.

And, in the matchup of the adventurer and the militant – that is, in the debate between the Nietzschean individualist who achieves his own salvation by defending the helpless and, by contrast, the disciplined intellectual who eclipses himself behind the party and would never, but never, take credit for the victories of the proletariat – it is ultimately impossible to say which wins out in Stéphane.

But such is the fate of those very special books that, since the Surrealists, have been called cult classics and that have enormous power to change lives. The experience of reading them counts for as much as their content. And what their readers make them say, the manner in which they shine in the minds of the young people who discover them, the transvaluation of the ideals that had held sway in their lives but that now suddenly seem obsolete or, the other way around, become exalted – all that is more important than what the books really said.

* * *

Portrait of the Adventurer was first of all an invitation to go on a voyage.

In the preparatory courses for France's *grandes écoles,* we were taught that there were two types of voyage.

The voyage of Ulysses, or that of Aeneas.

The voyager who thinks of nothing but his return, or the one who is constantly departing.

The one who remembers Ithaca, or the one who does not know that he will come to found Alba Longa, let alone Rome, the Eternal City.

The one whose voyage is a return to a lost city, or the one who voyages toward a city unaware it has been promised him.

The distinction is clear in Book II of *The Aeneid,* where Hector appears in a dream to Aeneas, revealing that his destiny is not a return to his hearth, as it was for the Achaean Ulysses, but endless wandering toward an unknown land.

It is generally from the second type of voyager that the adventures of the characters who fascinated Stéphane sprang.

It is that voyager who stirs in Lawrence as the young aesthete and apprentice archaeologist sets out for the desert.

It is he whom Malraux is mulling over when he sends Claude Vannec and Perken out searching for a royal road that appears on maps as a dark line striating a large white blot that is itself dotted with blue points corresponding to lost cities or unexplored ancient temples.

It is he whom Joseph Conrad, one of the models of Malraux and Lawrence, has in mind when, at the beginning of *Heart of Darkness,* he tells of his childhood passion for maps, of the notorious "blank spaces" indicating virgin lands whose "delightful mystery" fed his dreams of glory and into which, once he grew up, he would plunge, never to return.

It is he who is embodied by the voyager par excellence, the man with heels of wind, the one whom Stéphane implied was the master of all the others, the boss, Arthur Rimbaud: the voyage into hell, more demanding than the journey into night . . . the "today I know how to hail beauty" that sounded like a first farewell . . . and the sudden rush toward the "lost climates" of Aden, then Harar, from which he will return only to die . . .

And it is he whom some of us had in mind during a decidedly paradoxical adolescence in which we prepared for our entrance exams armed with the most coherent philosophical system that French thought had produced in a long time, but at the same time convinced that there was one and only one respectable destiny for the generation of students preceding ours at the École Normale Supérieure: the destiny, now forgotten, of Achille Chiesa, class of 1963, who stood out in Althusser's seminar on Lacan but then abandoned his pursuit of the agrégation to run off and bury himself in Thailand. We never really knew why; perhaps it was just because he was a cultural attaché . . .

I remember a dinner on the Rue Payenne at the home of André Pieyre de Mandiargues, a writer I wasn't crazy about. He had known André Breton, taken part in the resurrection of Lautréamont, crisscrossed Italy with Henri Cartier-Bresson, and inspired a film (*Girl on a Motorcycle*), a mixture of *Easy Rider* and *Romulus and the Sabines,* in which we saw Alain Delon carrying a naked Marianne Faithfull on a motorcycle. André Pieyre de Mandiargues is not read much anymore. Few remember his bibliophile's hands; the eyes, as diaphanous as those of an octopus, that sank into his cheeks; or the arrogance of a high lord but bad man who cut his contemporaries with his acid judgments. And few remain to evoke the love of pure literature of this deliberately minor author and his equivalent scorn for what he called *littéraille.* But I remember as if it were yesterday the end of that dinner in the fine apartment in the Hôtel de Marles, which looked out on the Musée Carnavalet. Before a hushed table of guests, Pieyre de Mandiargues improvised a dazzling commentary on René Char's poem, which was a revelation to me: "You were right to depart, Arthur Rimbaud."

I remember the conversations I had with my best friend at the time, future publisher Olivier Cohen. It was the winter of 1966–67, and we were in the thick of our preparatory classes at the Lycée Louis-le-Grand on the Rue Saint-Jacques.

I remember time spent talking between the *lycée* and the Place Saint-Michel metro station. When it was time to get home, we would charge, frozen, down the steps of the station. What would we talk about? Oh, the creation, in 1921, by Surrealist René Crevel of a stillborn review called *Aventure.* Or the mysterious fate of another Surrealist, Arthur Cravan, a performance artist and boxer who left almost no work behind when he disappeared into the Gulf of

Mexico. Or *The Treasure of the Sierra Madre* by B. Traven, another prototype of Stéphane's adventurer; we could not believe that Traven had not attracted more interest from the Surrealists, with the exception of Antonin Artaud. Or a scandalous misunderstanding, which amounted to an insult to the spirit of adventure that we valued almost as much as that of philosophy: all the "bourgeois newspapers" continued to view Pierre Mac Orlan as one of the masters of the genre because he had written *A Handbook for the Perfect Adventurer,* whereas he had interviewed Mussolini in 1925, signed Henri Massis's 1935 petition on Ethiopia, and then became an apologist for collaboration!

I remember (and recently learned that Olivier Cohen remembers even more clearly!) taking off that year in a pathetic attempt to flee (Rimbaud again) "the stupidity of Paris's poets," the "buzzing of a sterile bee" suggested by pacing one's room, and the already confining atmosphere of "bars full of pissing poets": a night train for Marseille; a berth on a cargo ship leaving for Tangiers; a head full of *The Secrets of the Red Sea* by Henry de Monfreid, another author not in vogue; the vertigo of daring to do this; the feeling of colossal transgression; my interception several hours before boarding by port authorities alerted by my family; and the pitiful return to Louis-le-Grand, where I had to answer questions, avoid people's gaze, and live with the shame and pride of this abortive adventure.

And then of course there was the day, several years later, when I set out for good "on the great dry and dusty road" to embrace the "rugged reality" of Bangladesh. It still wasn't the anchors aweigh of Lawrence and Rimbaud. Nor, perhaps, Nizan's for Aden. But I left without any real plans of return, alienated from my universities, my well-plotted professorial career, and my family. Once the war of independence had ended, I would spend months in Dhaka, in the chaos of a newly formed country and the seat of its nascent government, becoming involved in planning related to wells to be dug and malnourished children to be saved, and in the fate of the tens of thousands of young women raped during the war by Pakistani soldiers. I suggested to the country's first prime minister to treat those women not as pariahs but as *birangona,* or national heroines. All that is recounted in detail in the documentary film due to appear around the time this book is published.

Time has passed.

I am no longer the young man who could spend months away from everything – no telephone, no money, communicating with home via ultra-light airmail stationery-cum-envelopes that took eight days to arrive. No more am I the young man who was adopted by a Muslim family in the city's Segun Bagicha neighborhood, a family whose oldest son, now a brilliant software engineer in California, contacted me last year after seeing information in the Bangladeshi press about my return to Jessore.

Since then my travels, and especially my reporting trips, have been better framed, limited in time, and facilitated by contacts on the ground. Most important of all: the article to be written is always foremost in my mind.

But there is, in the latitude for improvisation that I always allow myself; in the promptness with which, once on the ground, I take advantage of the first opportunity to go off on a tangent and stray from the paths charted out (more or less) in advance; in the excitement I feel at the idea of being one of the few, since the evacuation of the American forces, to risk entering the no-man's-land that

Mogadishu has become; in the painful joy I experience in hunkering down for several days in the fetid trenches of Donetsk and Luhansk in Ukraine—here is found a wisp of my youthful dreams, a nostalgia for the great voyage, and, as at the moment I discovered *Portrait of the Adventurer,* a wholly intact yearning for parts unknown.

I remember a conversation I had in late summer 2000 with Edwy Plenel, then managing editor at *Le Monde,* to whom I proposed a series of articles on forgotten wars.

He didn't much like the idea that there might be wars that France's newspaper of record had "forgotten."

And it would take me a few days to demonstrate to Plenel and publisher Jean-Marie Colombani—by furnishing ample documentation to support my case—that there had in fact been quite a few wars over the years, even long ones with casualties numbering in the tens of thousands, to which their newspaper had devoted no more than brief notice.

Wars that appeared to make no sense . . .

Wars without promise, coherence, or climax . . .

Wars waged without aid of any of the great narratives that supply meaning; wars seemingly devoid of purpose, ideology, or memory, though they had sometimes ground on for decades without resolution . . .

But there was one argument that day that convinced Plenel, a fellow admirer of Conrad and Traven—and a former Trotskyite.

Do you remember, I asked him, those famous "blank spots" on the map where adventurers of yore wanted to be the first, and maybe the last, to visit?

And you are aware, aren't you, of the standard line about the approaching time of a finite world, the shrinking of its unknown lands, and the confiscation of the planet by all-powerful technology and communication?

Well, what I'm calling "forgotten wars" is a metaphor for that.

The forgotten wars are the equivalent – not geographically but politically and morally – of the blank spots on the map.

For what is a reporting trip of this sort if not a dive into the unknown?

Doesn't the reporter travel not only the serpentine rivers of Conrad, but also serpentine roads leading into dark places where there remain only ruins, corpses, and anxious people doing their best to survive?

And, today, wouldn't Conrad's Marlow and Malraux's Claude Vannec go out to meet the savages of another sort who, after torturing the wretched of Angola, Burundi, Colombia, the Nuba Mountains, or the parts of Sri Lanka controlled by the Tamil Tigers and their regiments of child soldiers, blanket their killing in silence?

* * *

In 2021, we are still not even close to this.

Putting aside adventure, blank spots on the map, and Aeneas versus Ulysses, it is the art of reporting itself that threatens to disappear.

And our era, caught between yesterday's mad consumerism and tomorrow's ecological solipsism, seems to offer only two choices to those still inclined to do reporting or simply to travel.

On the one hand, there are trips packaged by tour operators: tourism for the purpose of visiting monuments, having sex, or resting up – and sometimes journalistic tourism.

On the other, there is the chorus – which has swelled into a fanfare with the pandemic – placing the act of travel among the worst possible things people can do today, among the most repellent, most polluting, most anti-nature, most pro-carbon footprint, most inappropriate, and most clueless.

All the more reason then.

Under the circumstances, I am all the more determined to defy the cantors intoning the war on air travel and the return of each to his or her niche.

It is with an enthusiasm amplified by the internationalist demands of justice and brotherhood that I defy the new egoists, and thus the new reactionaries, who see the voyager – Ulysses and Aeneas alike – as selfish and smug, branded a criminal against the climate and humanity, a deviant amid the new global sanitary order – in short, as someone who strays from the new straight and orthodox thinking.

And just as Mallarmé exclaimed, "We have dealt a blow to verse," I do reporting to raise an alert: we have dealt a blow to travel! We are striking not only at the sacred duty to approach the afflicted, the wretched, the sacrificed, but also at the fair right of each of us to come and go, to return or not to return, to venture the voyage! If there is truly any aberration in that, if one wishes to see in it deviation or pollution, well, then, sign me up. I agree to be one of those polluters who cast off by the side of the road not their plastic containers or dead pets but their comfort. I say: "I love travel; I love it short or long, with or without a return plan; I love the irresponsibility of the fragile, undocked subject who is the true voyager, perpetually surprised and surprising!"

One who changes his locale, the Talmud says, changes his *mazal.*

One who changes his lodestar—or the arrangement of the stars over his head—can, despite what the idolators believe, write his own destiny.

And he commits himself—as Michel Leiris would confirm on the threshold of his departure for Africa, vying with Joshua as the latter was busy stopping the sun—to a poetic adventure in which the stake is, by traveling through space, to exert opposition until time bends.

That, too, is part of the beauty of voyaging.

That, too, on top of the duty of brotherhood, is one of its eminent virtues.

It is the consummate circumstance in which one must depend on oneself, in which one shrugs off his importance, and in which one stands a chance, a small chance, of gaining distance from himself and becoming a little bit "other."

It is the moment when Paul Claudel, standing before the Chinese pagodas and Japanese torii, ceases to be "His Excellency, the Ambassador," breaks with the plump, bourgeois, conservative poet he also is and, yielding to his own spirit, goes as mad as Tête d'Or, as mad as Rodrigo screaming, at the end of *The Satin Slipper,* "Free the captive souls," as mad as the crazy love in *Break of Noon.*

It is the moment when Malraux's Perken asks the English doctor in *The Royal Way,* using very nearly the same words as Lingard in Conrad's *Rescue,* "Have you heard of Perken?" and realizes from the expression on the doctor's face that here he is no longer anybody or anything; that no one knows him, recognizes him, sees him; that he has lost all status, all distinction, and any assurance of safety; that people mispronounce his name, chip away at his dignity, jostle him, look at him, when he passes, either with indifference or with a vague air of hostility; that neither his name nor his reputation counts for anything any longer, only the reputation of the country with which he is more or less identified; in short, that he is cut off, as in *Tête d'Or,* from the "character he plays in the world."

And as for the writer-reporter who makes it a point of honor never to conceal his identity and refuses to don a khaki jacket, cargo pants, and combat boots in order to "fit in" and feel "more comfortable"; as for the committed voyager, determined to be neither a functionary of his paper nor the colonist on duty who pretends to bring himself into unison with others and stand at their level – well, now he discovers that his inner compasses have gone awry, that his habits and certainties no longer do him any good. Here he stands in drenching rain or chalky dust, in maddening winds or blinding sandstorms. Here he is in the bed of a bumpy Toyota pickup choked by its exhaust. He breathes; he revives; he has remained the same only to discover the extent to which he could become another; it is the moment of a wayfaring subjectivization during which he simultaneously experiences his fragility and mourns the loss of his acquaintance with himself. What better way to bid farewell to the crowned Narcissus that is the true king of our era.

On the road, said Kerouac and his vagabond angels.

On the road, said T. E. Lawrence to his Brough Superior motorcycle.

On the road, much earlier, said Chateaubriand, the first of a great line of literary travelers who would return from far away with their forebears' *Atala* and Indian nocturnes tucked into their bags.

On the road, turn to the East, howled Tête d'Or, that conqueror more Rimbaudian than Shakespearean, who is the true point of contact between Claudel and the prisoner on a forced march, the walker of roads, and the definitive vagabond that was Arthur Rimbaud.

And Cendrars, after all!

And Baudelaire, the perpetual child captivated by maps and prints that transported him "far from the city's black and sordid sea": "Train, bear me; take me, ship, to other climes!"

And Louis Aragon, ever faithful to the young man he was when, with André Breton, he was discovering Rimbaud and Lautréamont—that lovely apostrophe, furious and mysterious, mouthed by one of the characters in *Les Voyageurs de l'Impériale:* "People are the same everywhere—a perpetual reason to flee!"

That is what they wanted to say, each in his own language.

The power of the voyage as the art of shifting oneself, of the reclassification and transformation of the world into a space available not only for the work of the mind but also for the actions of the body.

The minute trace of a single person, lost in the immensity of a world less finite and less round than it had appeared.

The magical fact that we discover and come to know ourselves through travel only when we no longer recognize ourselves.

The school of humility.

And it is because this way of thinking, which was already in a bad state, collapsed under the weight of the global house arrest imposed in reaction to the coronavirus that I decided, at age seventy-two—and as I have done all my life—to take to the road.

4

THE ADVENTURER

A Self-Portrait

But Roger Stéphane's book struck a second chord in me: It was an invitation to action.

The writers he profiled (Malraux, Lawrence, and others) were not the first or only members of their species.

And without dwelling on writers who were warlords (Laclos), arms dealers (Beaumarchais), or mercenaries (d'Annunzio); without dwelling on soldiers who were true writers (de Gaulle), who won literary honors (Winston Churchill), and who may not have known whether they were a man of arms or a memoirist (Caesar), the toppler of Carthage or historian of Rome (Cato the Elder), author of the battle of Fontenoy or of a posthumous treatise on military art with a title that echoed Rousseau (Maurice de Saxe, *Mes Rêveries*), the history of philosophy itself, including the most abstract, most speculative, and most classical of its components, is full of people who thought about the way one wages war and also were, in real life, authentic men of action.

The most emblematic case is the Plato of Letter VII, in which he offers his services to the tyrant of Syracuse, who our preparatory professor, François Chatelet, argued was as great as the Plato of the *Laws*.

Then there was Aristotle, who made Plato's dream come true when he became Alexander's tutor and gave him an annotated copy of *The Iliad,* which the young conqueror kept for the rest of his life at his bedside, next to his sword.

And Leibniz, a diplomat and spy for German princes.

And Descartes, whom we wrongly reduce to a dry mind busy with ratiocinations on cognition, method, dioptrics, or the passions of the soul. There is another Descartes, Professor Chatelet explained to us in a tone so reverent it suggested longing. One who fights duels, who enlists as a young man in several European armies at the start of the Thirty Years' War, who admires the military prowess of the prince of Nassau and hones his own scientific knowledge in the military academy that Nassau founded; one who travels in Bavaria, Italy, Sweden, and Moravia; one who, on the boat bringing him back from Holland, fights with the sailors who want to rob and kill him; one who perhaps read *Don Quixote;* and one who lives the philosophical adventure like a battle, a *charge,* requiring as much bravery as it does wisdom. On that score, his model is the audacity of Publius Decius, hero of ancient Rome celebrated by Livy, who threw himself through enemy lines in the hope of either achieving victory or dying covered in glory.

Whether philosophers or writers, many men of letters have been tempted to take up arms – or, even if they were not tempted, have been forced to do so by their times.

But what distinguishes the writers in *Portrait of the Adventurer* is not that they did this *and* that, not that they were writers and, by choice or by force of circumstance, *also* adventurers, and not that they accorded an *equal* dignity to writing and action, as did Thucydides and Polybius. No, what sets them apart is that they were drawn to reverse the equation, to reevaluate everything, and, for the first time, to give *primacy* to what they did over what they wrote.

Malraux in Spain really believed, according to the account of his companion in arms, Paul Nothomb, which I gathered for *Adventures on the Freedom Road,* that organizing and commanding an air squadron was more important than writing *Man's Hope.*

Lawrence was convinced that nothing meant more than participating in a great Arab revolt in which he led a small contingent against an army of fifty thousand Turks. And when he undertook to relate these lofty doings in *The Seven Pillars of Wisdom,* it was almost casually, starting with losing the first version of his manuscript while changing trains in December 1919. Then, six years later (Aeneas having turned into Ulysses and returned home), an overweening vanity led him to state on his application for reenlistment in the Royal Air Force that he was "administratively illiterate"!

Until the appearance of *Questionnaire* after the Second World War, Ernst von Salomon seemed to attach more importance to his work as an insurance agent, a money changer, or a banker than to his own destiny as a man of letters.

As for Rimbaud, whose shadow loomed over Stéphane's book, his farewell to words, his renunciation of poetry, his decision to hide from his youthful renown using the disguise that was most likely to erase it altogether (or else, as Claudel believed, to enhance it by means of a contrary legend), he went so far as to become a slave merchant and arms dealer with a "furious look," "dark skin," and "iron" body.

And finally, one last name that I was surprised Stéphane hadn't mentioned in our first encounter on the Rue Ernest Psichari, though it seemed obvious to me that not only Lawrence but also Malraux and even Rimbaud must certainly have remembered: Byron! Yes, Byron leaving Venice and its delights in February 1823 to go fight in Greece. Byron breaking the Turkish blockade and arriving in Missolonghi harbor several weeks later in the full uniform of a British army colonel, his helmet engraved with his coat of arms. Byron repairing the city's fortifications, raising a private army, buying arms, bringing in cannons, training artillerymen. Byron, a sort of generalissimo of the armies of free Greece, spending most of his time, from a mud house that stank of dead rats and fever, sending his battalions to the fronts at Vonitsa, Arta, and Agrafa. Byron plotting, between engagements, a new battle of Lepanto – yes, Lepanto, the same name as the big one that, two and a half centuries earlier, halted Ottoman expansion into Europe, the restaging of which was to be his masterpiece. Byron to whom, in the last weeks of his life, the assembled chiefs, Metaxa, Colocotroni, Mavrocordato, and Odysseus, offered full civil and military powers, an offer he clearly would have accepted had he not been felled by his final bout of fever. Byron the man who nearly was king and who came a half century before Kipling; a century before Edmund Musgrave Barttelot, the mad officer on the expedition that went looking for Emin Pasha and who served as Conrad's model for Kurtz in *Heart of Darkness;* a quarter century before James Brooke, rajah of Sarawak, Borneo, inspired *Lord Jim;* before Perken, of course, hero of *The Royal Way;* before Marie-Charles David de Mayréna, a model for the young Malraux, who devoted beautiful pages of his *Anti-memoirs* to the conquistador who landed in French Indochina and crowned himself king of Sedang. Byron, then, who preceded everyone else as the prototype of the adventurer-king who, if only for his own example, should have as much standing as the philosopher-king in the hall of mirrors of European consciousness. And finally, the same Byron who wrote, in a letter to his friend, Irish poet Thomas Moore, that should "fortune permit it to me" and should he live "ten more years," he would devote that time not to literature, which "is nothing" and which he no longer saw as his calling, but to his new vocation as an uncrowned king.

* * *

All that is not me, of course.

Without going so far as to believe, like André Gide in the famous scene recounted by Léon Blum in which Bernard Lazare approaches him to join the campaign to defend Dreyfus, that there is "nothing above literature," I rank literature very highly.

And in the great debate that divides the Greek world (which adds more to man's greatness, the act performed or its literary recounting, Achilles or Homer, hero or bard?), as in the inner dispute we know from Malraux that Lawrence never really settled (to bring us out of the murky night of invisible men and to leave some trace on human memory, is it better to be Alexander or Plutarch, or even Quintus Curtius Rufus?), my response has always been: the bard, of course; literature, without any doubt, for without books there is no memory; no Coriolanus without Plutarch. And that is why, because I have the privilege of being a writer, I did not wait long after the wars in Bosnia or in Libya not only to publish my war journals (*Le Lys et la Cendre* and *La Guerre sans l'Aimer,* respectively) but also to make documentary films (*Bosna!* and *The Oath of To-*

bruk). In so doing, I was no doubt running the risk of yielding to what Michel Butel has mockingly called "the lyre effect" – in reference to *The Iliad,* where under the amazed eyes of Patroclus, seated nearby in the shadows, Achilles begins to sing in his tent of the exploits of the Achaeans and himself. At least literature had the last word.

* * *

And yet . . .

How can we not acknowledge that once again things are more complicated than they might seem and that a dialectic keeps us constantly oscillating between the two positions?

How can I avoid confessing that when I bring together tribal leaders from all over Libya at a ruined farm outside Benghazi and have them endorse an "Appeal" scribbled on endpapers from a paperback edition of Aragon's collected poems, Roger Stéphane's paradigm is present in my mind?

And when I bring this or that warlord to Paris, when I suggest transforming a road in Jabal Nafusa into a landing strip for the clandestine delivery of arms, or when I sketch on a cafeteria napkin the plan of attack on Tripoli from Misrata, why has it not occurred to my adversaries not to point out my mimicry not so much of Malraux but of the adventurer of Missolonghi?

In a life that is beginning to feel long, I have made several documentaries and filed many, many reports.

Some were more in-depth than others.

At the request of President Jacques Chirac I spent several months in Afghanistan in 2002 as his special envoy, whereas two years earlier I had stayed in Angola for just a few days.

While investigating the death of Daniel Pearl, I made numerous trips to Pakistan, all rather long, while fifteen years earlier I did not see the need to spend more than a night in Harar, Ethiopia, where a bad guidebook had sold me on the supposed house of Rimbaud.

In Israel, I took the time to watch so many wars approaching, softly, like a spring breeze. And in the Tenga forest of Burundi, war crashed down on me like a thunderbolt.

I have searched for the dead in Darfur and found them without looking in Sri Lanka.

I spent successive winters in Bosnia, but lacked the time to travel to Armenia during the war in Nagorno-Karabakh.

And when I reread my eight recent reports, I have no trouble distinguishing a situation (Syrian Kurdistan) where I verified, after two tries, Alfred de Vigny's observation in his *Journal* that "a country is revealed in a single glance" from another (the Moria migrant camp on Lesbos) where, to fully understand, I had not only to stay a while, but to return twice. Or yet another (Libya) in which I spent less time, because of the ambush, than the tragic situation seemed to require, whereas elsewhere (Iraqi Kurdistan) I lingered a bit, even though the case deserved, in the view of the experts, no more than regional attention. And Somalia, where I quickly grasped that, in the pile of ruins that the country had become, there was not much left to grasp. And Donbass, where I needed time – and long spells of boredom – before being able to capture on film the joyful smile that belonged to Marta, a young lieutenant who served as my interpreter; or Alexei's awful groan of horror and anger as, gripping the bar of his bed in the field hospital, his sheets wet with sweat and blood, he tried to force his words out after being hit by a sniper's bullet that morning; or the evacuation of a body in a plastic casket, dangling from a helicopter's cable. And Nigeria: only a few days in I encountered Jumai Victor lying on her husband's grave: dried tears, empty eyes, no sighs, ready to die in her turn.

But one characteristic is common to all these scenes.

They speak to my secret program.

Each and every time, stretching back fifty years, I have had the ulterior motive of doing two things at once: not only to tell a story, but also to see that the story, when it appears, has an effect.

When Françoise Giroud, Jacques Attali, Marek Halter, Robert Sebbag, Italian radical Marco Pannella, and I were setting into motion our Action Against Hunger organization – now one of the most powerful and effective European NGOs – there was nothing ulterior about my motive: in war-ravaged Eritrea, then in the throes of population displacements ordered by the red tyrant Mengistu, or with the early Médecins Sans Frontières in Cambodia organizing the March for Survival, I went in with the twin goal of supporting a convoy of food, medicines, and clothing *and* throwing myself into the breach to bring back a report.

And even though the intention is not as clearly stated in the eight pieces collected here, it was no less clear in my mind (and, I believe, in the minds of Hervé Gattegno and Olivier Royant, respectively the managing director and former editorial director at *Paris Match*, who gave me carte blanche). I would not have seen the same things, interviewed the same people, or written in the same way had I not, in nearly every case, harbored the same twin intention, had I not been imagining, from the start, subsequent and very different scenes, such as receptions in Washington for a delegation of Nigerian Christians and for the incarnation of enlightened Islam, Sheikh Hasina, the "Dame of Dhaka"; the conversation already described of the meeting between the commander in chief of the Syrian Democratic Forces, General Mazloum Kobani Abdi, and President Macron; or the decision by the city of Paris to name a street for Afghan commander Ahmad Shah Massoud in recognition of his role in the history of the twentieth century.

I realize that, in saying this, I risk encouraging the conspiracy theorists who, for decades, have exhausted themselves searching for the dark powers they believe drive everything I do.

I realize that I am adding fuel to the fire of paranoids and conspiracy theorists like Erdoğan, who accused me of having been the hidden force behind the 2013 coup that overthrew the Muslim Brotherhood in Egypt and replaced it with a junta led by Field Marshal el-Sisi.

And perhaps I am also putting my finger on one of the points that accounts for the hostility that has gathered, in the most insistent yet unthinking way, around what I represent—that is, toward what I am trying to do with my life.

Too bad.

Or perhaps: all the better.

First, because I have hardened myself, of necessity, in the face of the most extravagant calumny to the point where I now tolerate it rather well. And if by chance calumny winds up killing me, at least I'll know why I died—which is not the case for many, many people.

Second, because I also believe that the strength of that hostility is not unrelated to the fact that its proponents cannot (or refuse to) say what motivates it. Now, I am certainly not going to do it for them! It is not for me to reveal the truth about those who detest me. But, knowing that the people to whom that task falls will grumble about it, I won't mind giving them a little help.

Third, and most important, there is a grain of truth in that hostility, as there often is in extreme malevolence. Which is this: in spite of—or perhaps because of—the high esteem in which I hold this profession, despite the admiration I have for Malaparte of the *Corriere della Sera,* Camus of *Combat,* Albert Londres of *Le Matin* and *Le Petit Parisien,* and Gareth Jones revealing the genocide by famine perpetrated by Stalin in Ukraine in the early 1930s, it is perfectly true that I have never been a journalist and am still not one.

For what is journalism, at bottom?

There is a journalistic ethic whose first principle is that one must separate the facts from their interpretation and aim, as far as possible, for objectivity.

There is a *doctrine* of journalism whose appearance—like that of the rules of ethnology, anthropology, and of the social sciences and the humanities in general—is not merely coincidentally contemporaneous with quantum mechanics. The first edict of that doctrine is that one must do one's utmost to keep at arm's length the law that the observer, if only by observing, modifies what is being observed.

And because here, too, things are even more tangled, it cannot be ruled out that the religion of objectivity, the article of faith that good journalists avoid any intervention in what they're reporting on, has something to do with the modern cult of *impersonality,* which is itself not unconnected to Rimbaud's "I am another." Nor is it unconnected to the fine modern desire to anchor our gaze in something other than an "I" drunk to the dregs with the romantic imagination. Indeed, it is positively coupled with the process of liquidation of the subject that began with Mallarmé, made its way through Debussy, Cézanne, and Manet, arrived at structuralism, and culminated in the characters of the novels of Michel Houellebecq: shriveled, skinned, and reduced to almost nothing.

The doctrine of objectivity is not trivial.

It draws on fine and noble sources.

But from whatever angle I view it, it is not and cannot be my doctrine.

I turn myself into a journalist.

I disguise myself as a reporter because I believe in inquiry, investigation, putting a knife in the wound, and immersing myself in the core of an event.

And even though my main object is the jostling of large forces, of major causes, and great necessities, I believe I hold my own in supplying telling details, sketching faces, and presenting people's lived experience.

But I am not a journalist. The resemblance between my work and that profession is no more than that between an individual and his namesake – and for one simple reason.

I am not a journalist because my slant is the inverse of the journalist's: I never set out on a reporting trip without the firm intention of intervening in what I see and changing what I show.

I am not a journalist because, in Malaparte, for example, in that towering writer whose works are enriched by reporting work, I draw a distinction between two bodies of work: the Malaparte of the strictly journalistic texts, which, like *The Volga Rises in Europe*, stand back from the facts, depersonalize their descriptions, and are never interventionist; and the Malaparte of the novels, which contain moments where, like a good son of the great poets of previous centuries, he allows himself to depict the dance of death in the slums of Naples, Ante Palevic and his plate of oysters replaced by human eyes, or the unfortunates of Hamburg upon whom fell a hail of phosphorus bombs and who had to be buried up to their heads for fear that their bodies, if exposed to the open air, might become torches – an entire artistic eschatology in which, like Dante, he sets out to study the fate of the denizens of modern Purgatory.

And when I point out to a Nigerian Christian humanitarian, to a leader of the Syrian Kurds' revolution, to Ukrainian president Zelensky, or, long ago in a palace under rocket attack, to Bosnian president Izetbegović that I am "not a journalist but a writer," I do so not to obfuscate, wrangle a free pass to a front line closed to the press, or hide my intentions. Instead, it is because I get the issue out of the way and announce, straightaway, that I will be a reporter who will break the sacrosanct principle of nonintervention; who will do what he can, against all scientistic objectivism, to influence what he sees; and who will deem himself equal to the event only once he is certain that the probity of his account will not prevent him, upon his return, from advocating for those who put their trust in him.

My reasoning self believes that in so doing I kill two birds with one stone: isn't it a good way to correct whatever there might be of excessive subjectivity and anti-bourgeois egotism in my love of travel? Doesn't the temptation that all adventurers feel to fight, as Lawrence says in the first lines of the preface to *The Seven Pillars of Wisdom,* "for his own cause" find its antidote in that activism? And, inversely, when one is concerned for others and lands on Lesbos among the undocumented migrants of the Moria camp, what better guide than B. Traven's *The Death Ship,* which, unlike the nautical novels of Conrad, tells a story not from the perspective of the ship's bridge but from the hold, the next-to-last redoubt of a handful of men "without passports, without countries, exiles, damned, nameless, never born"—in other words, undocumented?

My philosopher self muses that there is in my approach to reporting a fresh illustration of the role played in my life by the 1960s, one of the tenets of which was that words and things, saying and doing, discursive events and wordless events, are woven into the same cloth and conspire in the same intrigue: Louis Althusser's "theoretical practice"; the *archi-écriture* (or "archi-texture") that Jacques Derrida said formed the silent watermark of natural things no less than cultural phenomena; Michel Foucault's "devices"; the "arrangements" of Félix Guattari and Gilles Deleuze; and, in all the children of that generation who grew up to be writers, a distinctive hesitation, a quiver, that prevents them from knowing whether they intend to live as they write or to write as they live.

And finally the Jew in me cannot help but recognize himself in the inability to report facts without matching them with a good and rightful action—dare I say a mitzvah—the ultimate purpose of which will be the repair of the world, the *tikkun olam*. Let me reassure my teachers of Judaism old and young, I am not mixing orders. I well know that the fire to which the Torah calls me is not the "I saw the fire! I saw the fire!" of Fabrice at Waterloo in Stendhal's *The Red and the Black*, but rather that of the hand-to-hand with the letters of the Torah—which I have yet to undertake. But I am Jewish enough to know that even if the hearts of kings are in God's hands, man is a partner in the work of Creation and that this *participatory* dimension means that a Jew can never be relieved of the world, but rather is invested with it. Another lesson from Levinas and his Judaism is one of doing and of action. The priority he gives ethics over optics. Samson's hair, which holds all of his strength and from which derives Samson's hold on history, gives him, the last of the ancient judges, his righteous power to topple the temple of the Philistines and to kill his captors and tormentors. And so my conviction that being Jewish today, affirming a Jewish uniqueness in these times of distress, consists more than ever in this: to reject the triumph of the power of numbers; to fight the fatalism that seeks to replace the gods of yesterday with the nothingness of tomorrow; to resist nihilism, the bedrock of which is the quest for impersonality that lends so much weight to the ideology of journalism—all tasks to which I apply myself when I report, the major business of which is to have an influence, however small, on the reality reported.

5

WAR AND PEACE

A last word.

And a final clarification.

Some of the pieces collected here are war reporting.

I have filed countless such reports over the course of my life—from every continent on the globe.

But the fact is, as I've often emphasized and want to reiterate here:

I don't like war.

I don't like the literature of war.

I find Apollinaire's "God, how beautiful war is!" abominable. The same goes for Proust's evocation in *The Past Recaptured* of the magical Paris sky during the night bombings of 1917.

Not to mention Barrès's *Chronique de la Grande Guerre,* Péguy's patriotic odes and their poetic flights, or Ernst Jünger's appalling *Storm of Steel,* which would have been a Nazi book even if the author hadn't become one!

I reject the very idea that war can be poetic.

Even more strongly do I reject the idea that it can be a passage to greatness.

I prefer the view of Saint-Exupéry, an author I don't cite very often but who knew what he was talking about, who wrote in *Night Flight* that war is not an adventure but a sickness, like typhus.

I prefer Malraux's insistence that no one in this world deserves more respect than one who is capable of waging, and winning, war without loving it.

I prefer Hector's initial retreat from furious Achilles, who is foaming at the mouth and screaming that he's going to eat Hector alive and throw his remains to his dogs – and the fact Hector steps up only upon realizing that Athena has tricked him and that his choice is to fight or die without glory.

Achilles is best at the point in *The Aeneid* when Ulysses finds him in hell and has him admit that, all things considered, he would have preferred to be a man without a country rather than the too-powerful warrior he was, wading in the mud of endless battles and reigning now over the dead.

I prefer peace.

In the wars I covered, only the sad, shining moments of relief and fatigue after the guns had gone quiet have captured my love.

In liberated cities, I have treasured the moments when, with the acrid smell of the fighting still hanging in the air, people stop glancing with a worried eye at the last building at the top of the avenue on the left; when, in Mosul, people stop pulling their lapels over the tiny crosses around their neck; when people in Bujumbura cease feeling like they're in someone else's game.

In Sarajevo, I loved filming women as they resumed putting on makeup, teachers going back to teaching, students studying, filmmakers filming, and writers writing.

In Benghazi, I treasured the day in August 2011, after Qaddafi's fall, when the only shots you heard were celebratory.

I love reading war histories – but starting at the end.

I love the periods of peace that punctuated the Hundred Years' War; the peace that ended the Thirty Years' War; the Peace of Longjumeau and Saint-Germain between Catholics and Protestants; the multiple truces and treaties of Prague and The Hague; the Peace of Vervins between France and Spain; Cornwallis's surrender at Yorktown; the Treaty of Appomattox.

I love the peace of the French at Verdun and the English at the Somme, with their round helmets, their dreaming faces, their overcoats caked with mud.

I love the peace on the exhausted faces of the ancient Greeks, bloody and naked, swords sheathed.

I love the moment in *The Iliad* when the Greeks and Trojans agree to settle their differences through a one-on-one combat between Menelaus and Paris. Alas! Paris, having been seduced by Aphrodite, flees. But how happy they all were! How loudly they hailed with hands and voice, Achaeans and Trojans alike, the end of that eternal war.

I love the Peace of Philocrates between Athens and Macedon; the peace after Thermopylae; the truces of the Peloponnesian War.

I love the peace in the faces of poets whose eyes have lost their terrible epic glow, who have begun to dream again of giving meaning to the world and its people.

After the fighting ends, the world ends, everything ends, I love the fraternization of tired soldiers, of forlorn generals consumed, like Pyrrhus, with smoldering regret, and I love that they find themselves sitting out in the open at the edge of a field littered with steaming corpses.

I love the fact that "peace" is the most beautiful word in every language and in Hebrew is one of God's names.

I love Hölderlin's celebration of peace, "heavenly, softly echoing," with its "cloud of joy," its "ripe fruits" and "gold-wreathed cups."

I love the French Festival of the Federation held on July 14, 1790, before the sun of the Revolution had become stained with the blood of the Terror and gave way to the world-shaking, irradiant, and terrible sun of Austerlitz.

I almost love the peace of the Jews at the Hôtel Lutetia in Paris in 1945: the peace of tears and desolation, the peace where one discovers that *he* is not on any of the busses in the convoy, that *she* will probably never return, and where, nevertheless, the survivors count each other, the shipwrecked souls breathe again, and what remains of life timidly reclaims its rights. It is dismal, this peace, tasting of ashes. It is despicable that none of the returned are allowed to say that they have gazed on Gorgon. It is almost unbearable that children return to playing without trembling, that people recover their speech and return to their routines—*as if nothing had happened!* But one cannot fail to love that moment of peace.

I love nothing more, actually, than pacifism.

True pacifism.

The pacifism of Romain Rolland, Stefan Zweig, lovers of civilization, higher understanding, and hope.

The pacifism of Norman Mailer, in the last interview he gave me just before he died in 2005, when the novelist of *The Naked and the Dead* proclaimed his opposition to the absurd, useless, devastating war in Iraq.

And it cannot be said often enough how great this kind of pacifism is, gentle pacifism, the celebration of peace that the Talmud makes into a prayer for the empire, the kingdom: nothing on the spiritual, philosophical, or political plane is its equal. It shames and censures the Jüngers of the world and their paeans to the German soldier and his sacrifice, the Marinettis of "Futurism" and its pre-fascist cartoon violence, and even the Surrealists and their fistfights, real or feigned.

And never can I praise too highly the pacifists who embrace this peace: their peace is the greatest of battles, the most heroic of conquests, the most imaginative of visions of the future. For cement, for mortar, for its cornerstones and foundation stones, this peace has no more and no less than man's spirit. And that spirit, projected into civilization, transcending nations and languages in paradoxical, impossible, radiant concert—*that,* I would like to be able to show once and for all, is what is most beautiful in the world.

But I also know there are just wars.

And I know there are times—for example, when defenseless people are massacred—that for love of peace and true pacifism one must resign oneself to war.

I know it from Saint Thomas, Francisco de Vitoria, and Saint Augustine, all Christian theoreticians of legitimate war—that is, the type of war that does not add war to war but rather subtracts war from war.

I know it from Martin Walser, the lay theoretician of just and unjust wars.

But I also know it from having heard it from the mouths of my elders concerning the war in Spain, followed by the war against Hitler, which had to be fought.

And I know it, too, from having lived it.

Once you have talked, negotiated, tried everything; once the adversary has led you around and toyed with your scrupulous diplomats, you must make war: on Milošević to stop the war against the people of Kosovo; on Qaddafi threatening to drown Benghazi in rivers of blood; on the Islamic State when it marches on Erbil and sows death in Europe. I know, yes, that sometimes the beast declares war on the spirit, or barbarism on the beauty of the world, and in such cases there is no other choice but to rise to the challenge and, using all one's strength, wrench the crown from low-browed Heliogabalus.

I detest that the marvelous Jean Giono of *Horseman on the Roof,* that model of ease and Stendhal-like grace, that ally of courage in the face of the scourges, falsehoods, and horrors of death in the time of cholera, did not demonstrate these same good reflexes when another plague, the brown plague, descended on Europe and Giono leapt into the arms of German power.

I detest the Giraudoux who, when Gentle France began to welcome the humblest of the humble, the most disinherited of the disinherited (that is, the Jews of eastern Europe), calmly declared war on them, whereas when Hitler and his legions were gearing up he did not think of war at all but rather unconditional peace, appeasement. He took it lying down. Worse, he wrote and staged his atrocious pseudo-Greek play, *The Trojan War Will Not Take Place,* in which he converts the great Hector into a French veteran, an appeaser before the fact. "Repugnant" was Claudel's word for the playwright's "apologia for cowardice" and "peace at any price."

Naturally, I detest Céline playing it brave and bold when, after the war, he depicted himself facing off against journalist Pierre Dumayet, he as a watchdog baying the alert against rising danger. At the moment of greatest danger, when France was a desert, he had never stopped repeating, with a sadistic fierceness, that sounding the alert made no sense, that resistance was absurd, and that the only course was to accept the logic of arms and the law of the survival of the fittest.

I despise Handke for having put his talent in the service of Greater Serbia and its ethnic cleansing.

I feel sorry for Michel Onfray for having suggested in 2015 that France come to terms with ISIS in order to "preserve the peace" and "calm the young soldiers of the Islamic State who are in our suburbs."

I regret that our languages lack separate words for victorious peace and shameful peace: the peace of May 8, 1945, versus the Franco-German agreement signed at Montoire on November 16, 1940.

All that, too, is a sort of pacifism.

But it is not cast from the same metal.

It is of a softer, coarser, baser material.

It is transient while the other is noble; resentful while the other is generous; spineless while Romain Rolland and Stefan Zweig are brave; blind while the other is lucid.

It is, in fact, the exact opposite of the first.

And this baser form of pacifism, the pacifism of perfidy and unprincipled compromise, I despise as much as I love the other, and I condemn its twin, bellicosity.

I do not support the ideology of zero-death wars, which is its most recent form.

Nor do I believe that refusing to kill is the right response when Herostratus becomes master of the world.

I often wonder about the cause of all that confusion. What accounts for the resignation of democrats, whose weakness strengthens dictators? Whence the widespread repudiation of the concept of humanitarian intervention and responsibility to protect, which, when formulated in the latter half of the twentieth century by French doctors like Bernard Kouchner and American thinkers like Samantha Power, was a noble step forward?

Because the world is sick of violence? Really?

Because we've had enough brutality, cruelty, hate, and their processions of informers and denigrators?

No, alas.

For never, in fact, has hate been so powerful.

Never has denunciation been so loud or so proud.

Instead of it being tyrants who order the denunciations, it is individuals: each of us monitoring our neighbor with a fierceness worthy of a tyrant, informing on him, outing him, turning him in. But the result is scarcely different from the form of denunciation encouraged by tyrants: bitterness, rancor, and anger are at their peak—alas, not the kind of anger that enlarges individuals and peoples; not the proud anger of the Greeks, which Aristotle said, in the *Nicomachean Ethics,* was provoked by injustice! No, the other kind, the kind the Greeks called *thumos,* which made Plato's Callicles so bad. The kind that Saint John Chrysostom later explained as follows: if God locked that anger within our breast, it is because it is "like a fierce beast that, were it not locked in, would tear us apart." The kind whose modern names are nihilism and resentment.

No.

I see in the repudiation of courage something else – and, once again, its opposite.

I see in it an ironclad indifference to the pesky poor people who are the subject of this book.

I see the sign of a world where one side is closing its gates to the other, in which the grim reaper harvests names and places.

I see disdain for modest little lives, too small to have a history, an archive, a face on our smartphone screens, or a place in a John Steinbeck novel.

And I also see – forgive me – hate for what was noble about ancient heroism; scorn for the figure of the Christian knight who saved what deserved to be saved in the figure of the pagan demigod and embodying the other facet of the religion of charity, was a welcome supplement to its concern for the widow, the orphan, lepers, small children, and Mary Magdalene; hate for what was great in the great Jews who were Samson, Saul at war with the Amalekites, Esau slaying Nimrod, David the poet king, and Rabbi Akiba swept up in the iron nets of the Roman legions because he wanted to continue studying during proscribed hours, believing it beneficial for humankind; hate, in a word, for what there is in man that is a little greater than man; hate for man as a bridge and not a destination; hate for what Nietzsche, who understood pretty well the greatness of Hellenism, Christianity, and Judaism, had the reckless candor to call the *superman.*

My God!

What a lot of hate in the world.

What a lot of hate among the legions of the falsely indignant on the right and on the left.

Among the outraged multitudes of the far left and those of the far right.

What a lot of hate in ordered minds, much more terrifying, when really rigid, than a police order!

What a lot of hate in the death row that Western societies resemble when they succumb to depression, paranoia, and suspicion.

I have written against that hate.

I devoted a book, *The Virus in the Age of Madness,* to the animosity that masquerades as love, able to say only, "Take your ticket, get vaccinated, keep your distance, distrust each other, assume the person next to you is infected."

And it is for the same reason that I preferred not to merge with an antiseptic society reminiscent of *The Elegance of the Hedgehog,* a society that claims to repair the living, valuing only the quotidian hero (preferably caregivers). I preferred to stand apart from this movement, which, from the being-for-death of the philosophers, fashioned specters to haunt supermarket aisles in search of masks, sanitary wipes, and hydrogen peroxide. Instead, I spent a year traveling to the front lines of the Islamic State, to the miasmas of beautiful, breathless Bangladesh, and to a Kurdistan fighting with the energy of the losing side.

And it is for this reason that I battle here to remind, plead, demonstrate that there are just wars, that people are needed to fight those just wars, and that still others are needed to witness and report on them.

PART TWO
ON THE ROAD

6

NIGERIA'S CHRISTIANS ARE UNDER SIEGE!

Nigeria, November 2019

It's happening in Nigeria, Africa's largest economy.

It's a slow-motion war, horrific in its cruelty, with a large and mounting number of victims killed or displaced.

It's a massacre of Christians on a scale that appears to exceed even what the Christians of the Middle East have undergone.

And the world pays no attention.

Few in the United States or Europe have reported on it.

A Nigerian Pentecostalist Christian alerted me. He is a professor in Lagos, Nigeria's economic capital, and director of a nongovernmental organization working for mutual understanding between Nigeria's two largest faith communities, Christians and Muslims: at thirty-six, his manner has something of the easy, ironic elegance of Barack Obama.

"Have you heard of the Fulani?" he asks me at our first meeting, speaking the flawless, melodious English of the Nigerian elite. "Officially, they are charming shepherds with a long lineage in the Sahel. They are reported to move south with their herds in search of greener pastures, after being forced out of the north by climate change. But in fact they are Islamic extremists of a new stripe, loosely linked with Boko Haram. The Global Terrorism Index ranked them, in 2015, among the four most deadly jihadist movements, right behind ISIS, the Taliban, and Boko Haram. If you don't believe me, come. I beg you, come and see for yourself."

Knowing, of course, of Boko Haram, the extremist sect entrenched in the mountains and forests of Borno state in Nigeria's northeastern region, but nothing of the Fulani, I accepted his invitation.

I traveled to Godogodo, Kaduna state, in the very center of the country, where I filmed the account of a beautiful young woman named Jumai Victor, who was missing one arm, though this was not immediately noticeable because of her off-center way of standing sideways. It was the night of July 15, she says . . . The Fulani storm in on their long-saddle motorcycles, three to a bike, shouting, "Allahu Akbar." They torch houses. Kill her four children before her eyes. When her turn comes and they notice she is pregnant, a discussion ensues: some do not want to see her belly slit, so they compromise by cutting up her arm with a machete, like butchers, starting with the fingers, then the hand, then the forearm, then the rest, after the last one in the group complains that he has not had his chance. She recounts her story speedily, without visible emotion, staring into space, as if she lost her face when she lost her arm. It is the village chief, translating for her, who chokes up. It is he who has tears streaming down his cheeks when she finishes her account.

I ventured farther north to Adan, in the chieftainship of Kagoro, where I recorded the tale of another woman, Lyndia David, who has survived another massacre. On the morning of March 15, rumors reach her village that the Fulani are raiding in the vicinity. She is dressing for church as her husband prepares to go into the hills with a group of other men to stand watch. He urges her to take refuge at her sister's home in a neighboring village. On her first night there she is awakened by the whistles of the sentinels. Once outside the house, she sees flames spreading around her. She tries to flee: a Fulani blocks her path. She reverses direction: she is stopped by another Fulani. Another direction: another Fulani. They're everywhere, a tightening trap. Then she hears a voice speaking in her own language. "This way," says the luring voice. "Come this way, you can get through!" Trusting the voice, she runs toward her savior, who leaps out of the underbrush and assaults her, cutting three fingers from her right hand, carving the nape of her neck with his machete, and shooting her point-blank. Thinking her dead or dying, he then douses her body with gasoline and sets her afire. A few weeks later, her body still an open wound, a true survivor, she makes it back to her village and discovers that, on the same night, the Fulani leveled it, killing seventy-two, including her husband.

In Daku, near Jos, capital of the Christian Middle Belt, a country of blooming prairies that once were the delight of the English colonizers, I visited a vandalized church, its corrugated metal roof collapsed, a heap of cold cinders where the cross had stood.

I spotted another church, intact, on the outskirts of Jos, its square baking in the heat but alive with veiled girls dressed in white. A man emerges, yelling at me that I have no business being there. He speaks English. Stalling, I am able to learn that he is Turkish and a member of a "religious mutual assistance group" that is opening madrassas for the daughters of Fulani in the northern and central parts of the country.

—

That day, with an escort provided by the neighboring district, I crisscross a strip of the Middle Belt within a radius of about thirty kilometers. Crumbled roads. Collapsed bridges. Destroyed houses casting broken shadows in which, between a smoldering straw pallet, a pail, and a kitchen tool, one sees trails of black ash and blood. Nothing left of the trees but stumps. And, in the abandoned fields, maize rots on the stalk because not a single Christian soul is left alive – or because those still living are too terrorized to come and harvest it. In the distance, there are clusters of white smudges. They are the animals for which the villagers were driven off. They are the herds of the Fulani grazing on the lush grass. The landscape suddenly seems so vast . . . When we approach, the armed shepherds repel us with hand gestures – I am not able, for the moment, to get a word out of them.

The bishop of Jos has had his livestock stolen on three occasions. In the course of the third raid, he was dragged into his room, a gun to his head, and was saved only by his faith: dropping to his knees, his eyes shut tight, he prayed at the top of his voice until the thrumming of a helicopter drowned out his chant and drove his assailants off. He recounts for me the unvarying pattern of what appears more and more to be an ethnic and religious cleansing.

The Fulani arrive most often at night. They are barefoot – so when they are not on their motorcycles you cannot hear them coming. Sometimes a dog sounds the alert. Sometimes, when the attack occurs during the day, it is a sentinel. And then: a terrifying stampede, whirling clouds of dust, wild cries, as if the invaders are trying to encourage each other. And then: before the villagers can take shelter or flee, the Fulani are upon them, in their houses, swinging their machetes, chasing cries in the night, seeking out pregnant women, burning, pillaging, raping. They do not always kill everyone. At a given moment they stop. They recite a verse from the Koran, round up the terrified livestock, and go out the same way they came in, hastily, leaving the dead to the wolves. Survivors are needed to tell the tale, to spread fear from village to village, to bear witness that the Fulani, fearing nothing but Allah, are capable of anything.

The heads of seventeen Christian communities have come down to Abuja, Nigeria's federal capital, to meet me in a nondescript compound on the outskirts of the city. Some of them have traveled for several days in packed busses or minivans. Some are late because they had to get around the checkpoints that are part of the state of emergency in the states of Yobe and Adamawa, traveling at night. Reaching the outskirts of Abuja, which some of them had never seen before, they melted into the crowds. But arrive they did, each accompanied by one or two victims. And here they are, an exhausted yet earnestly hopeful group of forty-odd women and men keenly aware of the gravity of the moment, full of expectation. One carries a USB key, another a handwritten account, a third a folder full of photos, captioned and dated. These they intend to release like messages in a bottle dropped, not into the sea, but into the hands of a stranger whom they know nothing about except that perhaps he will be the messenger and the mouthpiece of their suffering. I accept these records. I peruse these documents. I am overwhelmed by the weight of the bearers' hope and by the task they are entrusting to me. What if these packets of words, these loose sheets, these crude photos are the stem cell of the memorial in which the horrors they have experienced will someday have to be preserved?

For the time being, taking the floor in turn, these survivors of hell confirm the modus operandi described by the bishop of Jos.

Starting with the victims, whose empty expressions seem to say that they are dead even if we perceive them as living, each adds an awful detail to my bumper crop of atrocities. The mutilated cadavers of women. The mute man commanded to deny his faith and then cut up with a machete so as to extract from him at least a scream. A girl strangled with the chain of her crucifix. Another broken against a tree at the entrance to her hamlet. And in each case, the banality of an evil whose grip on pastoralists who are, like them, among the wretched of the earth, they cannot comprehend: is it by order of the radical mosques that are springing up as fast as the churches burn down? Is it ancestral Fula supremacy whipped to a frenzy by malign shepherds? Or is it merely the savagery of man, resurfacing in response to an evil spell?

At any rate, I realize that this is a real true war being carried out by the Fulani. In it I see an enlarged Boko Haram. An extended, rampant Boko Haram. A Boko Haram offshored, relocated, multiplied from village to village. A Boko Haram crossing borders behind which the world believes it had been contained and that is now sowing the seeds of murder everywhere. In short, a forest of Fulani crimes concealed by the tree of Boko Haram, and no one seems to be aware . . . The two are unmistakably linked, of course. An American humanitarian told me of internships for Fulani volunteers in the bush of Borno state. An Italian priest recounted that Boko Haram "instructors" have been spotted in Bauchi state, where they are teaching Fulani elites to handle weapons that will replace their machetes. But the Fulani, let us be clear, do not have borders. They are Boko Haram no longer confined to a bastion equal to 4–5 percent of Nigerian territory. The Fulani represent the savagery of Boko

Haram extended to all of the unbelievers, Christian and Muslim alike, of Nigeria, Chad, Niger, Cameroon, and beyond.

Often, in the villages to the west of Jos, on the way to Kafanchan, I asked to see the weapons the villagers use to defend themselves: bows, slings, daggers, sticks, leather whips, and spears. And would you believe it? Even these makeshift arms have to be concealed, because when the army comes through after the attacks, the villagers are told, "These are against the law," and their paltry defenses are confiscated.

On several occasions I noted the proximity of a military base that might have been expected to protect civilians against these bush marauders. But the soldiers did not come. Or if they did, it was only after the battle. Or they claimed not to have received the SOS calls in time, or not to have had orders to respond, or to have been delayed on an impassable road.

"What do you expect?" exclaims our driver as we take off in convoy toward Daku and his burned-down church. "The army is in league with the Fulani. They go hand in hand. A few years back, in Byei, after an attack, we even found a dog tag and a uniform."

"It's hardly surprising," adds Dalyop Salomon Mwantiri, one of the few lawyers in the region who dares to represent the victims. "The high command of the Nigerian army is Fulani. The whole administration is Fulani. And President Buhari, an African blend of Erdoğan and Mohammad bin Salman, an ex-dictator who already took power, from 1983 to 1985, through a coup d'état and who depends on subsidies from Ankara and Qatar, is a Fulani."

This complicity was confirmed a few weeks ago in Riyom district, at the expense of four displaced persons who, attempting to return home, were gunned down near Vwak. The villagers know the assailants. The police identified them. Everyone knows that they took refuge after the attack in the village of Fass, two kilometers away. But there they are under the protection of the Ardos, a sort of local Fulani emir. No arrests occurred.

The complicity was also confirmed, according to Sunday Abdu, the traditional village chief of the Irigwe in Bassa district, on the occasion of the attack on Nkiedonwhro. This time, the military came to warn the village of a threat. But they ordered the women and children to take shelter in a school. Once they had done so, one of the soldiers fired a shot in the air, as if giving a signal. A second shot sounded in the distance, as if in response. A few minutes later, after the soldiers had departed – supposedly to pursue the suspected assailants, according to the officers involved – those assailants appeared, went directly to the classroom, and fired into the cowering group.

I traveled on to Kwi, farther to the south, to reflect at the graves of three young men buried the day before. The incident took place on April 20. The dead youngsters, wielding sticks, have just fought off a Fulani attack. The police, showing up, as usual, a minute too late, do not pursue the attackers but instead take the young defenders and fourteen of their neighbors into custody on charges of having perpetrated "inter-community violence." The fourteen resurface soon enough, though not before being copiously tortured at police headquarters. But the other three cannot be found. And only after several weeks do the villagers learn the truth. They had been separated from the others early on and killed. Their bodies were offered to ECWA, Jos's largest hospital. And for weeks medical students, with the blessing of the authorities, performed anatomical exercises on their dismembered remains, preserved in formaldehyde and kept on ice. "Dispose of them any way you want," said the police representative when the hospital returned what was left of the bodies following multiple inquests and autopsies demanded by the villagers. "But if you bury them, no plaques or crosses – by request of the Ardos!"

I also met some Fulani.

The first time, it was by chance. I was with my photographer and an interpreter in an unescorted Toyota taking us to Godogodo. Arriving at a destroyed bridge, we have to descend into the riverbed to pick up an unpaved track. Climbing back up the bank, we come upon a checkpoint consisting of a rope stretched across the road and a hut in which two armed men are dozing. "No passage" is the message conveyed to us by the younger of the two, who wears a jacket on which are sewn badges in Arabic and Turkish. "This is Fulani land, the holy land of Usman dan Fodio, our king – and you whites can't come in." This memory of King Fodio, whose conquests, two centuries ago, led to the establishment of the caliphate of Sokoto over the Fula and Hausa lands, I thought persisted only in North Africa, but apparently not. We are several hundred kilometers south. And this dream of an Islamic state built on the bodies of animists, Christians, and Muslims resistant to radicalization is being emulated here.

The second encounter was on the outskirts of Abuja. Driving toward the countryside, just after Lugbe, we come upon a village that is nothing like the others we had seen in the Christian zone. A ditch. Behind the ditch, a hedge of bushes and pilings. The air of being closed off from the world. And instead of houses, huts from which emerge a swarm of children and their mothers, covered from head to foot. We are in a village of sedentary Fulani. We are amid nomads who, once the enemy has cleared out, do not hesitate to carry out a tiny, localized Fulanization. "What are you doing here?" demands an adolescent who comes out of nowhere wearing a T-shirt adorned with a huge swastika, while we are feigning interest in a field of red chili peppers. "Are you taking advantage of the fact that it's Friday and we're in the mosque to come spy on our women? The Koran forbids that!" When I ask him whether wearing a swastika on his chest is not also contrary to the teachings of the Koran, he is momentarily puzzled before launching into a feverish tirade, the conclusion of which is pretty clear: he is perfectly aware of wearing "a German insignia"; but, except for "bad souls" who "hate Muslims," he believes that "all men are brothers."

Later I encountered Fulani in Lagos, at the southern extreme of the country. Upon leaving the outermost band of the city, in an area reached after hours of walking or, what amounts to the same thing, of "go-slow," the name for the monstrous traffic jams that literally choke the city, one finds an open-air market where the Fulani sell their livestock. I am with three young Christians, survivors of a Middle Belt massacre who live in a camp for displaced persons. They pretend to be cousins, coming to buy a fine animal in preparation for a family feast. And while they are negotiating over a white-horned pygmy goat (a half hour to bargain down from 1,600 to 1,200 dollars, then another half hour to get the seller to agree that the buyers will not take delivery until the following day), I go in search of Fulani who are willing to talk. That day, most of them have come from Jigawa state on the Niger border, crossing the country from north to south in trucks to bring their stock here. And though I do not succeed in learning much about their trip, I have no trouble getting them to express the joy they feel in being here, on the border of this contemptible promised land, both vile and delectable, ready to carry out the orders of their emirs and finally be able to "dip the Koran in the sea." There are "too many Christians in Lagos," says Abadallah, the most talkative of those I meet. "The Christians are dogs and children of dogs. You say Christians. To us, they are traitors. They adopted the religion of the whites. There is no place here for friends of the whites, who are impure." The shepherds around him chime in, appearing convinced. The postcard vendor who joins the group and offers me portraits of Erdoğan and Osama bin Laden agrees that the Christians will eventually leave and that, *Insha Allah,* Nigeria can finally be "free."

Now, of course, some professional disinformers will try to reduce the violence occurring here to one of the "interethnic wars" that inflame the African continent.

And I suppose they will find, here or there, acts of reprisal against the Fula and Hausa tribes.

But on the tail end of this trip, I have the terrible feeling of being transported back to 2007, when the horsemen of Khartoum sowed death in the villages of Darfur; or, further back, in South Sudan, before the death of John Garang precipitated the war of the Islamists against the Christians; or, still earlier, in Rwanda, in the spring of 1994, when no one wanted to believe that the fourth genocide of the twentieth century was getting underway.

Will we let history repeat itself in Nigeria?

Shall we wait, as usual, for the disaster to be done before waking up?

And will we stand by idly as international Islamic extremism, contained in Asia, combated in Europe, defeated in Syria and Iraq, opens a new front across this vast land where the children of Abraham have coexisted for so long?

These are the stakes behind my voyage to the heart of Nigeria's darkness.

This is the meaning of the campaign to save Nigeria's Christians that I hope I am launching today.

7

NIGHT OF THE KURDS

Kurdistan, December 2019

They're held here, the French nationals who fought with the Islamic State, in this modern prison in Derik, south of Qamishli, the capital of Syrian Kurdistan. A Turkish missile has landed close by, as if to persuade the detainees to flee. But the prison holds on. The guards are helmeted, masked, dressed in black. And you can't gain access to the top-security section without passing through a series of corridors, fences, and armor-plated doors. A dozen inmates are gathered together at the end of the cell, backs turned as we arrive, praying. At the call of the guard stationed at the peephole, they turn as one and I find myself face-to-face with jihadists who are, I am told, among the most vicious assassins of Raqqa. But in this cell so brightly lit that no shadows are cast, a cell that smells like an old basement full of piles of bedding in garish colors, they look more like poor wrecks in dirty sweatpants and polo shirts, weary-eyed, resigned. Except for one who was wounded when his legs got caught in a scrap metal trap, who shouts at me in his northern French accent, "We know who you are!" This is followed by a clamor of pitiful complaints along the lines of "Do you know who is going to try us and when?" These monsters who terrorized the world are now cut off from everything. Deprived of daylight, of cell phones, of the single television set that was taken away when the Turkish offensive began in October 2019, they do not know, for example, that al-Baghdadi, their leader, is dead. At this moment, they have but one thing in mind. To be extradited from Rojava, not to end up in Baghdad to face capital punishment. To return to France, the homeland of the rights of man and the right to a legal defense. Pathetic. And frightening.

A few kilometers away is a second prison. This one is for children. In reality, it's a sort of cloister lined with arcades and only recently converted into a correctional facility. In it we find a hundred-odd adolescents, all boys, who, like Nelson from New York or little Ahmed from Toulouse, say they've never committed any crime except to have a father or mother who was a terrorist. They are like small, hunted animals. Many of them don't know whether their parents are alive or dead. And they have that air of desolate anxiety that is the hallmark of children forever deprived of a future. We are led straightaway into a closed room where two French kids await us, their eyes fixed on the ground for most of the interview. One, an eight-year-old, tells us how he used the skills he acquired from pulling the eyes out of the cats in the souk in his village to cut the throat of a neighbor who showed disrespect for his older sister. The other, who has an angelic face with lovely gray eyes and an empty look, would gather the heads that his father, an executioner in Raqqa, cut off. My God, how does one react to confessions like this? What form of deradicalization, what redemption, can be possible for such monstrous children? Might not the worst crime of the Islamic State be that of having attempted to make of these "lion cubs" the transmitters of a plague of villainy that will be passed from generation to generation? I ask the second one, the apprentice gravedigger, if he ever thinks about those faces without bodies, if he ever dreams of them at night. He asks me to repeat the question. Then he looks at me for the first time, but with an air of undefinable stupidity. He no longer knows what it means to dream.

Kurdistan is her nom de guerre. She is a tiny woman, pretty, her hair in braids. She commands a battalion of about a hundred women stationed somewhere near the front line. When we arrive at dawn, the soldiers are busy with calisthenics. But she leads us into a building where, with a handful of her comrades sitting around her on the floor beside their Kalashnikovs, a rug laid over the bare cement to keep out the morning cold, she begins her account. Speaking in a measured, musical voice, she tells us how her unit faced the Turkish invasion. The noise of aircraft covering the advance of the infantry of killers from Afrin. The two wounded soldiers whom they rescued from the road, under fire. The young heroine, whose memory haunts her, shot point-blank on the outskirts of Tal Abyad. And then the moment when they realized that the Americans were really going to leave and that the unit would have to fall back to save what could be saved of Rojava and gain time to plan a counterattack. I think of the women warriors of *The Iliad* who protected the cities. I think of Penthesilea, queen of the Amazons, who loves Achilles, engages him in one-to-one combat, and, in Kleist's version, succeeds in killing him. The difference is that these young women do not love their enemy or anyone else. These warriors are married to Rojava as the monials are to Christ. No seduction, no passion: the lay puritanism of an order of Antigones who watch over the eleven thousand kinsmen and kinswomen killed in the war against the Islamic State – and now against Erdoğan.

It is said of the Kurds that they have no friends but the mountains. Here in Syrian Kurdistan, with its plains, its half-built, meandering villages, and its makeshift oil wells, they don't even have mountains. Does that mean that here they have no friends at all? In Qamishli, in the overheated offices of the Autonomous Administration of North and East Syria, I pose the question to Fawza Youssef, writer, feminist, and member of the collective leadership of Rojava. Not at all, she says, and now I'm paraphrasing her response: "The democracies are our friends. Civil societies are our friends. And this society, our society, the society that we are in the process of building, is another friend. It's an egalitarian society. It doesn't draw religious or racial distinctions. And, in opposition to the old patriarchy revived by radical Islam, it puts women and men on the same footing." Fawza is not a Marxist. But she is very well aware – she proclaims this with a burst of laughter that softens a beautiful face marked by militant, passionate, and tough struggle – of the debate in the West over the end of communism and of Rojava's reputation for harboring one of its last variants. But you don't have to be a Marxist, of course, to put liberty, equality, and fraternity side by side. And it is this blend of horizontality and Spartan zeal, of libertarian spirit and revolutionary discipline, of ecological communalism and internationalism, that is the core of Rojava and the soul of its resistance.

Aldar Khalil has no official position. He is one of the many veterans among this people in arms who, since 2011, have been building this republic of equals. And, he assures me with a gesture of the one hand he still has, he is just one of many who inspired the coalition of Kurdish parties that calls itself the Movement for a Democratic Society. But from the respect that everyone shows him, from the haste with which the sentinels folded up their backgammon game the moment he arrived, and from the hint of false modesty he shows when he concedes that, yes, perhaps, from time to time, he might offer a recommendation here or an instruction there, I understand that things are more complicated and that, in Rojava's actual structure, within the Invisible Committee where no one, in principle, is better than the rest, he often has the last word. Unlike Fawza, he received Marxist training. He is also the only one of our Kurdish interlocutors to proudly acknowledge the link with the PKK in Turkey. And when he mentions, and justifies, the switching of alliances that Syria's Kurds had to accept after being abandoned by the Americans and left with their backs to the wall, he makes me think of Lenin in Isaac Babel's phrase: the Lenin who, unlike Blaise Pascal's God, draws a curve with a straight line. The same unbendable will. The same cold analysis of the mechanics of events. And the same dialectical flair in rationalizing, like Lenin in Brest Litovsk, the bitter compromise with Bashar al-Assad and Putin.

"Hello, General, what is the situation on the ground?" The staticky voice on the phone is that of a young president calling from a capital gripped by the Yellow Jacket strikes to spend forty minutes of his time worrying about the state of the Kurdish forces and about what they need from France. The general, Mazloum Kobani Abdi, is the commander in chief of the Kurdish army and the source of the famous quote: "Between genocide (Erdoğan) and compromise (Bashar), we choose life." From the day he said that, Turkish drones have tracked and targeted him wherever he is reported to be. And we are there, crowded around my iPhone and a volunteer interpreter in the best-connected corner of the most unlikely site (half disused hotel, half abandoned Club Med copycat), where the meeting and the call were to be held. He appeared just after nightfall, unarmed, accompanied by two of his officers, at the top of an absurd stairway that led nowhere. It is not my place to summarize the substance of the exchange between Emmanuel Macron and Ankara's public enemy number one. But if Aldar is the hidden Lenin of Rojava and Fawza its Kollontai, Mazloum is its Trotsky. And among the points under discussion with Syria, there is one that falls into his bailiwick, the nonnegotiable status of which he took great pains to emphasize to his French friend that night, despite two dropped connections, in a voice made even more solemn by the surrounding darkness. That point is the autonomy of his army, the maintenance of its chain of command, and the assurance that it will occupy itself solely with the defense of Rojava and not become involved in any dirty battle (in Idlib, for example) organized by the criminals against humanity in Damascus. Of that essential condition, imposed as a point of honor, France took note that night.

On the other side of the Tigris, in the other Kurdistan, Iraqi Kurdistan, ISIS is back. Forty kilometers north of Erbil, we are on the ridge of the Qara Chokh range, which has been the Peshmerga's highest position since October 2017 when, in the wake of the Kurds' referendum on self-determination, General Qassim Suleimani's pro-Iranian militias pushed the Kurds out of the "disputed" territories. And yes, ISIS is there below us, eight hundred meters away. A mortar shell landed here an hour ago. Followed by a sniper shot that grazed the roof of the bunkers. And we could even see, until the mist settled into the valley, two suspicious-looking pickups on a deserted track. General Sirwan Barzani doesn't seem all that surprised. He reminds us – while watching a large bird turning with only the slightest movements of its wings and swooping into the hollows before quickly rising again toward the sea of clouds – of his prediction: that the jihadists would not fail to fill the void left by the forced retreat of the Kurds. And so here he is again, the tycoon condottiere, the founder and president of the thriving Kurdish telecommunications company Korek Telecom, spending his days and nights here, in the rough, with his men, standing guard against the barbarians. It is this civic heroism that I have always admired among the Peshmerga. I revere this corps of citizen-soldiers composed of men of all ages and stations, the lords of the Barzan hills commingling with the simplest farmers, faces dark with the week-old growth of beards, coming out of the Kurdish night. And it is this same worried but joyous fellowship that, thanks to my friend Sirwan, I find again here today.

Was the idea approved by Washington? Or was it on his own initiative that Steve Fagin, the American consul general in Iraqi Kurdistan, organized a screening of my 2016 documentary, *Peshmerga*, in the bunkerized mini–Green Zone in Ankawa, the Christian quarter of central Erbil, where the U.S. forces are headquartered? I'll never know the answer. But there can be no doubt about the emotions shared during the most dramatic scenes of the film: Maghdid Harki, the young white-haired general, unhelmeted, facing ISIS, struck down by a bullet to the head; Ala Tayyeb, my cameraman, stepping on a mine and shattering his shoulder; or the battalion of women mounting an assault on the Mosul dam. I know that there, in that improvised theater, are Special Forces commanders. Agents of the CIA. Seasoned diplomats hardened by the immoralities of realpolitik. But when the lights come up after the film, all in attendance seem to display the same touch of embarrassment and perhaps of remorse: always, in every war, free men get blood on their hands; but usually it is the blood of their enemies; whereas here, in Kurdistan, it is that of their friends, of their bravest and most loyal allies. How could the nation of generals John Pershing and George Patton, the world's oldest democracy, succumb to such an act of self-betrayal?

When my documentary was made, Masoud Barzani was Kurdistan's president. He passed the torch to his brilliant nephew, Nechirvan, after the referendum. And now I find Masoud in the same palace where I had come to urge him to get the green light from the United States to enter ISIS-occupied Mosul, just as General de Gaulle did when he convinced Eisenhower to allow a French division to liberate Paris. He displays the same silent authority he always had. The same imposing presence, despite his small stature. And the same uniform and cap of the eternal Peshmerga. With, however, a new touch of bitterness tingeing his account of the battle of Altun Kupri, near Kirkuk, where one of his commanders was able, like Leonidas at Thermopylae, to hold back for several days an Iraqi force assisted by Iranian Revolutionary Guards and commanded, in person, by Qassim Suleimani. Or, even better, the battle of Shila, never spoken of in the West, where his troops destroyed fifty-seven armored vehicles. How is it possible that a battle of that scale could pass under the radar of history? Whatever the reason, I admire Masoud Barzani for being able, like the generals of the French revolutionary army, of the Israel Defense Forces, and of the early Soviet revolution, to stand up so superbly to the rest of the world. I admire his dignity, wandering his deserted palace like an old, fallen king, with nothing left but his pride and glory. And I admire the fact that, like Cincinnatus back behind his plow, or Camillus elevated to the status of a sage after saving Rome from the Gauls, he remains the father of his nation.

It's a scene from Dino Buzzati's *The Tartar Steppe* or Julien Gracq's *The Opposing Shore*. We are three hours east of Erbil, close to the Iranian border. It is here that the third Kurdistan, Iranian Kurdistan, known as Rojhelat, has exiled fighters serving in Peshmerga uniforms. Scattered over a landscape of craggy, menacing rock, stationed in stone shelters tirelessly refortified, and equipped with weapons repeatedly refurbished with a patience worthy of Sisyphus, we find a handful of men on perpetual alert who, for forty years, have been praying for the fall of the regime of the mullahs. The stakes are huge. These rearguard guerrillas, who never stop preparing for an assault that never comes, are among the most hardened of the Peshmerga. But this life of waiting, of stalled heroism, this anticipation of a confrontation constantly deferred, this succession of days during which weapons sleep and sentinels expire from shouting, "Who goes there?" to an invisible enemy, these endless nights when the watchmen go blind and come to resemble hermits atop their pillars, this motionless time during which the only things that fall are the snow in winter, the sun each day, and the wind, which, on good days, spreads over the mountain the illusion of a voice that might be that of six million brothers and sisters under the Iranian boot – all of that makes one desperate.

And then, suddenly, no longer is it the deserted Tartar steppe. The Iranian Revolutionary Guards on the other side, fed up with these tireless resisters and their clandestine incursions, decide to strike and to launch, as they did in September 2018, a salvo of missiles that fall here in Koya on the headquarters of PDK-I, of which the resisters in the mountains are the armed wing. We are in the small room in which the full executive board of the party, which had been meeting that day, sought refuge after the first missile hit—only to be struck a few seconds later by the second and third. Khalid Azizi, the party's secretary general, was miraculously spared because he had stayed behind in the boardroom to assist a wounded colleague. But the rest of the board was wiped out. Hanging on the walls of the memorial that this death chamber has become are the portraits of those killed. And, lovingly arranged in showcases along the walls, is a collection of their belongings: identity cards, sandals, cell phones, pairs of glasses, a comb, a watch, a packet of medicine, a pistol, a blood-stained turban, a medal. The Kurds are a forgotten people. But these Kurds, stranded on this particular opposing shore, who have made it a point of honor to faithfully reconstruct their phantom admiralty, are, with their brothers on the other shore—those hanged, tortured, and imprisoned between Mahabad and Mariwan—the most forgotten of the forgotten.

On the road back, in a village at the foot of the mountain, we come upon a makeshift bazaar piled high with odd lots of goods. There are computers, canned food, medications, hardware, diapers: everything that Iranian Kurdistan, starved by the regime and international sanctions, needs to stay alive. And men of all ages are piling these goods into rattletrap trucks that will set off up the mountain road. Because they then must traverse the Zagros ridge, carrying their bundles of misery and survival on their backs, these smugglers are called "kolbars": *kol* meaning back and *bar* meaning to carry. Reportedly there are tens of thousands of them throughout the province. But because they take the ultimate risks, defying icy paths and Iranian soldiers who fire on sight, because they remind us of the

Bosnians who supplied besieged Sarajevo over the Mount Igman trail and of the international brigades that crossed the French Pyrenees to fight for the Spanish Republic, we see them as resisters of a different sort. It is to one of them—a seventy-year-old man in mourning for his eldest son, who had been his companion on the trail and whom he had to leave up on the mountain, frozen in snow, as the winter set in—that I dedicate the last words of this trip through the three Kurdistans. Before the team of porters set out, he asked us: "Are my children's children, and their children, condemned to live like human ants? Will they continue to live life, to give life, and to die for these pieces of plastic and cardboard? How many generations will it take before their hope becomes something more than another burden to bear?" The Kurdish nation has paid too dearly for its endurance and for its unflinching dream of a Kurdistan that is independent, free, and open. Give the Kurds justice. It is time.

8

DONBASS

Trench Warfare Lives on in Europe

Ukraine, January 2020

The huge troop-transport helicopter dates from the Soviet era. It's flying low, just above the tree line, nose down, to avoid Russian radar. After two hours of flying over a landscape of smooth ground, frozen lakes, and villages in ruins, all of which emerges bit by bit through the night, we arrive in Mariupol. That's where the Ukrainian general staff has organized our first meeting, in the headquarters of the Navy Guard, with the officers who, for the last five years, have been leading the fight against pro-Russian separatists in the Donbass region. But I didn't wait for the briefing. And I hardly needed to see the satellite images of the three Russian cruisers blocking the passage between the Sea of Azov and the Black Sea (in defiance of international law) to gauge the state of things. The nearly deserted fish market in the center of town. The empty shops on Lenin Avenue. The enormous blast furnaces of the Azovstal factory running at half power and emitting thin clouds of dirty black smoke. Mariupol is one of Ukraine's largest cities. Before the war began, it generated nearly 10 percent of the country's GDP. But now the separatists, unable to take control of the city, have imposed a blockade and are slowly choking it to death.

Lying eleven kilometers farther east, Shyrokyne used to be Mariupol's seaside resort. This morning, all that remains of its two thousand residents are a couple of former hotel keepers who have come in under the protection of a national guard unit to lay flowers at the grave of a father who was hastily buried last year in the family plot. Of the formerly elegant houses that lined Shapotika and Pushkin Streets, nothing is left but piles of rubble that closely resemble the ruins that the pyrotechnicians of ISIS left behind in Iraq and Syria. Shyrokyne, insists Marta Shturma, the young lieutenant who will serve as our interpreter throughout the entire period of our reporting, was an ordinary resort. One need only walk along the coast, its waters now gray, to grasp that it had no strategic importance. So, the church with the collapsed roof; the clinic reduced to its concrete pillars and mined; the school pulverized by heavy artillery, where we find, as if after an earthquake, a section of blackboard, children's half-burned notebooks, and a backpack, miraculously spared – did the separatists destroy them just for the fun of it or out of spite for being made to cool their heels outside Mariupol for months? Was this the urbicidal vengeance of marauding irregulars who, before pulling back, were in the habit of burning down cities? For the sadistic joy of seeing the last inhabitants, like Maxime and Tatiana, the couple who returned this morning, fleeing under heavy fire? We are in Ukraine, and the year is 2020. Even so, it's easy to imagine an army of vandals who, failing to take New York, might lay waste to Coney Island.

But the war is not over. I am about to see proof of this thirty kilometers farther north in Novotroitske, where the tenth battalion of the mountain assault brigade is positioned. After leaving the highway, we spend an hour on a rough track in a fake-real armored ambulance covered with red crosses before arriving at the first outposts. We learn that, not far from here, a soldier was killed at 7:15 this morning and another wounded. We spend the rest of the morning with General Viktor Ganushchak and a special forces unit, weaving our way through an endless network of trenches, all zigzags and corners, like the streets of a buried city. Some are deep enough to resemble tunnels or caves; they are shored up with boards and logs. Others are open and hidden behind a curtain of artificial gray ivy; they offer protection only if you bend in two. Every fifty meters a sentinel sits, sometimes in a bunker heated by a coal stove that stings your eyes, and sometimes behind a lookout station lined with old straw. The officers are proud to show me this intricate and interlinked line of disciplined sentinels that will prevent any more breakthroughs like those that occurred during the lightning pro-Russian offensives of 2014 and 2015. I don't dare tell him that the sight of these exhausted men, their eyes swollen with insomnia, who are relieved only every six months and who, by virtue of pacing the same little patch of dirt, no longer know where they are, reminds me of a terribly archaic Verdun, frozen in time.

Krasnohorivka, which lies a few kilometers to the north, is practically adjacent to Donetsk, the capital of the self-proclaimed republic of the same name. And it is here, in fact, that the two soldiers were hit this morning. We passed through Marienka, which has been largely spared during the fighting, although last week a mother was targeted by a sniper while walking her child to school. We went to the town's church, standing intact above its stone steps: the faithful believe that the church's golden onion domes protected them from the hail of bombs. We covered the last few kilometers by spacing our vehicles well apart, since here the enemy is only a few hundred meters away. Maxime Marchenko, the unit's colonel, used the word *enemy*. For the duration of our journey, I will never hear him or any of his colleagues say "the separatists" or the "pro-Russians." Because, for them, the cause is clear: it's the Russians, not the pro-Russians, who are firing at them. "Look," the colonel says to me, pointing at what's left of a Grad missile. "Only the Kremlin has weapons like that. And come look at this . . . " We are climbing to the seventh floor of a government office building converted into a field headquarters and topped with a watchtower. There, using binoculars to see through an opening in a wall of sandbags, we make out the suburbs of Donetsk, an immense city that was long called Stalino. With its concrete housing blocks, its downtown factories, its slag heaps, and the metal carcasses of its destroyed airport, it's a Jurassic Park of sovietism. And there, in the foreground, stands a stationary convoy of Gvozdika tanks of the type used in the second Chechen war. True: it's pretty hard to imagine how they could have come from anywhere but Moscow's arsenals.

In the Myroliubovka zone, we are even farther north but not as close to the front. We come upon a firing range in which stand three 152 mm howitzers. As we watch twenty or so young Ukrainian artillerymen busying themselves around the mouths of the guns, the commanding officer hastens to tell us that this is just a drill. But he cannot help adding (and here I am paraphrasing): "Look at those steel monsters. Look at those men ready and able to load and unload the beast, calculate the firing angle, back up, reload, work the breech. We are a civilian army. We obey the orders of our commander in chief, President Zelensky. And unlike the enemy, we make it a point of honor to observe the cease-fire laid out in the Minsk accords. But I'll tell you one thing: If the strategy changes, if the general staff decides on a counter-offensive and orders us to free the lost territories of Luhansk and Donetsk, then Europe will see that this citizen army is a force to be reckoned with, one capable of winning this war." I cannot help thinking back five years, when Petro Poroshenko was president, to the battalion I saw on the outskirts of Kramatorsk, not far from here, which had just been savagely bombarded. That unit seemed so short of equipment and so vulnerable! I remember the soldiers, their faces etched with a deathly pallor, so exhausted they were sleeping standing up, leaning against the wall of the room where the president had called an emergency meeting of his officers – one even stood on crutches. What a long road to the situation before me now: six years in, a Ukraine standing tall on the shoulders of these tens of thousands of soldiers!

Pisky, still farther north but now within reach of Donetsk, has been completely destroyed – and mined. We had to enter it on foot in single file behind the patrol that came out to meet us. Not one building left standing. Bombed houses, including one where the empty windows had been boarded up, the boards hung in the shape of crosses. Two streets that looked like vacant lots, the dead grass competing with the new-fallen snow. No water. No power lines or sewers. Of the thousands of souls who had lived in the town before the onset of this madness, only three families remain, holed up in their basements. But the leader of the patrol hasn't seen them for weeks. Just possibly, he exclaims with a laugh and pretending to count on his fingers, there is no one left alive in this doomsday landscape except him, the Russian snipers who sneak in at night using infrared sights to kill their targets, and the few dozen men dug into the icy ground with their automatic weapons, invisible to us. Even the officer with the bleak sense of humor seems taken with the irreality of the place. Marta, our interpreter, speaks in a toneless, choked-up voice that echoes long in the cold air. We hear the faraway cries of sparrow hawks. We encounter a starving dog licking the edge of a stone well. Another lies dead on a pile of rubble, its paws stiff and its eyes glassy. Pisky is a ghost town. Men and beasts alike are specters. Nothing on our trip will scare me more than this gutted, lifeless landscape through which we move among pale, bloated shadows.

I don't know what came over me. Especially since one more cadaver won't make a difference in this war, which has already claimed thirteen thousand victims, and about ten more every week, despite the official freeze on the fighting. But I awoke this morning with an irrepressible need to learn more about the wounded soldier and his friend who was killed in Krasnohorivka the day before yesterday, at 7:15 a.m., just before our arrival. So we head to the field hospital in Pokrovsk to which they were evacuated. The fatality, Yevhen Shchurenko, is in the morgue, his head blown off, his body dressed in a new uniform, creating the appearance of a martyr. The wounded man is in a shared room with five other victims, civilians and soldiers, that week's casualties. In the bed opposite lies an adolescent who moans softly, as if trying to even out his pain. Another is inexplicably agitated, his lips coated with bloody saliva; the head doctor says that a bombardment drove him mad. The man we have come to see is silent at first. He has the feverish, absent look of those for whom nothing matters except to feel a little less pain. But then he decides to speak and, leaning on the side rail of his bed and carefully pulling back the sheet to show us the bandages on his abdomen and thigh, he tells us two things in a voice that is weak but steady. How he was hit by shrapnel just as he was jumping into the trench to man his post after morning duties. And that he had placed too much confidence in the European patrols that are supposed to be monitoring the cease-fire here in the war zone. This reminds me that we had seen two white OSCE (Organization for Security and Co-operation in Europe) cars pull up two hours later that same morning, at 10:30, just as we were getting ready to return to our ambulance, not far from the spot where the rocket hit. I also recall the sarcastic remark of an officer, addressed to no one in particular, that these "clowns" were supposed to have been here since dawn. Is there a link between A and B? Between the late arrival and the attack? And is it to check whether I had indeed come? Maybe.

Stanytsia Luhanska is at the north end of the front line, the last of the points the belligerents set up to allow Ukrainians on both sides of the line to cross from one zone to the other. To be precise, it is a corridor bisected by a metal fence with a sort of customs station on either side, separatists to the east, loyalists to the west. Except for one detail that is hard to miss. As we watch, barely anyone is moving into the separatist zone. Whereas in the other direction are endless lines of babushkas with shopping bags, wizened seniors being pushed along in wheelchairs, and young people who have lined up since dawn. When I ask about it, this is what I learn. Ukraine, which views the inhabitants of Luhansk and Donetsk as hostages of Putin and the separatists, still honors their rights as Ukrainian citizens, and continues to pay their pensions. Because the separatist governments are puppet regimes, on the other hand, these thousands of poor people must withdraw their money from ATMs at banks in loyalist Ukraine. The Jurassic Park image of Putin's putative green paradise that I first got from the watchtower in Krasnohorivka comes into clearer focus: the stores being empty on the separatist side, these people come to free Ukraine to spend their modest pensions on the staples they need for the month. To tell the truth, I can't see why they don't decide, once and for all, to spare themselves these grueling trips and settle on the other side. It occurs to me that their acceptance of this weekly ordeal may be the Putinized version of the old Soviet voluntary servitude. But who, in this war, is the hostage of whom? That is a question that one no longer needs to ask after seeing these long lines of migrants who are allowed to pass, with great difficulty, through the gates of their "separatist" prison.

In Zolote, which borders Luhansk, we encounter more trenches. Cruder that those of Novotroitske, they consist of little more than boards laid onto the dark ground. But they are more striking because of the huge dogs guarding the entrances, like so many Cerberuses at the gates of this hell of a war – and especially because of the overequipped Rambos, their faces darkened by dirt or tattoos or hoods, standing guard at points ten meters apart. They seem like professional soldiers lying in wait. Might they be members of the Azov and Aidar battalions, famous for their bravery and for having served, since 2014, as a hideout for ultra-nationalists and even neo-Nazis? No. Because I met with Azov's commander, Denis Prokopenko: his men were training in Mariupol. I saw Aidar's commander, Oleksandr Yakovenko: but in Kiev, where he told me that his 760 men were "on rotation." To be totally frank, it even crossed my mind that the new Ukrainian army, patriotic and overwhelmingly republican in spirit, might be quietly ridding itself of these extremist elements. No. These camouflaged troops – who seem raring to go, younger than those I have seen up to now, and noticeably more composed – are close combat pros, some with their knapsacks on the ground, others wearing them on their back. I am told that they have just been inspected by President Zelensky. These hypnotized commandos behind their wooden lookouts behind the line of brown earth opposite us that marks the enemy position are manning one of the defensive positions of Ukraine's national army. But it's easy to imagine, as at the firing range in Myroliubovka, that the position could be quickly converted into an attack base. Might it become one? Might Ukraine choose to recover, by force, its lost territories? Might it trade them one day for Crimea, the loss of which I suspect it has been silently grieving, as the Europeans once did? I don't know.

We are in Kiev with President Zelensky, sitting in the same ultra-kitschy office where I had sat so often when Petro Poroshenko was president. Around the faux marble table, he took the same seat as his predecessor had always occupied. He showed his adviser, Andriy Yermak, to the same seat that Poroshenko's sherpa of the moment had always assumed. And he invited Gilles Hertzog and me to take our usual places, so to speak, instilling in us a feeling of a past recaptured but shifted in time. As he pensively studies the photos of his army that we have taken for him, I see Poroshenko's massive silhouette superimposed over the body of the smaller and younger man who succeeded him as president. Was he cut out for the job? Is it possible for a comedian to mutate into the commander in chief of an army at war? Could he prove to be more than the sitcom actor whose election seemed to nearly everyone to be the apotheosis of the "society of spectacle"? I watch as he recognizes in each picture the stretch of the front where it was taken, and sometimes the officer. I listen as he worries about the European Union being weakened by its leniency toward Putin; listen as he simultaneously celebrates the solidity of his ties with the France of Emmanuel Macron. I note his mastery of official-speak as he turns to the dark American drama that he unwittingly triggered by a phone call with Trump. And I conclude that, all things considered, he is muddling through pretty well. Three times, perhaps to avoid a question, he repeats that he feels quite "normal" and that nothing could be more "normal" than answering questions about the present state of mind of the little Jew from Kryvyi Rih who became a television star and then president of this land of pogroms and blood that was Ukraine. Does he mean that he normalized himself by entering the club of world leaders? Or rather that he's still the same normal young guy he was when we first met before his surprising election? It really doesn't matter. Because predominant in him now is a sardonic and serene self-assurance that I had not expected to find and that causes me to think that history could have chosen a worse champion to stand up to Putin and his "Eurasiatic" imperialism and to defend the colors and the values of Europe. And, as for us heedless Westerners, this lost war in Ukraine – with its drip-feed of tragedies, and on this side of the five-hundred-kilometer front, these good people who continue to stand guard two hours before midnight – should not be forgotten. No, it should lie heavy on our collective conscience.

9

THE END OF THE WORLD IN MOGADISHU

Somalia, February 2020

First, the blue of the ocean. The bright white of the fishermen's houses. As perceived through the plane window, a sense of Italian languor. Fittingly, since, in the Somali language, *Mogadishu* means a tea garden for travelers. But, upon landing, a change of scenery. The airport is like a fortress, surrounded by Hesco barriers and tangled metal, into which the al-Shabaab jihadists poured mortar fire yesterday morning. Mistrustful custom officers don't question you about coronavirus but instead ask if you're armed. The city is nearly entirely destroyed, its collapsed buildings denuded of their concrete pillars and steel beams. And on the top level of the old Xooga Hospital, to which we are immediately led, we encounter this: kneeling above the void below, a government sharpshooter on the lookout for a rebel sniper spotted this morning by the neighborhood watch. "But hasn't al-Shabaab pulled out of the city?" I whisper to the sergeant standing a few feet off. "That's news to me," he answers, stifling a laugh. "Mogadishu is a sieve." He gestures as if shaking a dish rack. "The terrorists come and go as they please.

Even down there, in the hospital cemetery, they're waiting for the burial to begin." Below, under the spreading crown of a loblolly pine, I see a group of women milling about in their colorful *abayas*. A little farther on, men chatting in front of a tombstone. And, at the entrance to what looks like a vacant lot, a convoy of 4×4s, signifying the eminence of the deceased. But the sergeant herds us abruptly into the only part of the stairway still protected by a bit of roof. The government rifleman fires. A pickup behind the cemetery wall starts off in a cloud of red dust. When we come back down, the women under the tree have not budged.

Upon arriving in Mogadishu, the first problem is where to sleep. The Afrik Hotel was pulverized by a car bomb. The SYL was attacked for the third time in December. At the Sahafi International, which appeared in guides before the time of al-Shabaab, there was a firefight, and two French citizens were taken hostage. At the Central, the receptionist triggered her own bomb vest. At the Wehliye and the Siyad in the Green Zone near the presidential compound, things are hardly any better: two human bombs made it through the gates and blew themselves up. The truth is that the hotels have been systematically targeted. Because that's where, in this African Grozny, anyone resembling an international official or functionary might be bunkered up. The best solution is still this camp adjacent to the airport, where you rough it but at least you're out of the line of fire. Housed here, in modified containers protected by enormous anti-tank barriers made of packed sand, are the Ugandan and Burundi officers of the African Union mission (AMISOM) sent to support the transition government barricaded inside the Green Zone. Some junior diplomats and intelligence types. Italian special forces. The handful of Navy SEALs who stayed behind after the U.S.

Black Hawks were downed in 1993. A few hazily identified warlords. And the hundred "mentors" employed by Bancroft, a private American NGO reportedly funded by the U.S. State Department. They train AMISOM's elite commandos, managing a base straight out of a novel by Graham Greene or Gérard de Villiers.

Dawn departure for the front line of this curious war in which this mixed bag of an army sallies out to do battle with a force that is all the more fearsome for being unseizable, consisting only of shadows. A Ugandan colonel from the General Dhagabadan training camp commands our convoy. A Somali reconnaissance group takes the point, followed by a Burundi protection vehicle and an eleven-ton Casspir tank made in South Africa, into which we are packed in the stifling heat. Two VAB armored personnel carriers bring up the rear. Pulling out of the compound, we run through the latest instructions: watch out for homemade bombs laid down by al-Shabaab before the vehicles come through and controlled remotely by scouts on motorbikes. Beware of fake checkpoints set up overnight, like the one just a mile from the city that trapped the deputy commander of the Kahda district the day before yesterday. And the worst is the return trip, when you think you're out of danger, but there's only one route, which al-Shabaab probably mined after you passed on the way out—in which case: *boom!* We are issued bulletproof vests that come up to the chin. A stretch tourniquet that they show us how to tie above a wound. And a last piece of advice about the ingenuity of those experts in *burkubi,* meaning savage destruction, who can lay mines so that they go off only after they're crossed for the second or third time. To our left, through the rear window of the Casspir, lagoons and salt marshes. On the right, pitchy dunes and brush from which, the "medic" explains, no one can dislodge the world's first terrorists to have fused the models of al-Qaeda ("Islam has no territory") and ISIS (based in a hinterland run like a "caliphate"). Suddenly, up in the turret, the gunner spots a drone flying over the bush. Theoretically, al-Shabaab possesses only spy drones. But you never know. He fires. Hit, the drone spirals down through the calm, birdless sky.

Jazeera is supposed to be the last village on the coast under Somali control. Points beyond are controlled by al-Shabaab, with their public executions, stonings of adulterous women, and Islamic tribunals applying sharia law. The goal of our mission today is to be seen. In showing ourselves, we reassure villagers that they're on the right side. A half dozen government soldiers, armed to the teeth, go off in the sand hunting for intelligence, dwelling by dwelling, always fearful of coming upon a rigged house, but also needing to project a friendly and protective image: "What's new? Has al-Shabaab been back? Do you feel safe?" Another unit ventures out to the beach, where a fisherman with a face seared by salt and sun holds in his arms a tuna with huge gills. He's embarrassed when I ask him the price of his catch, thinking I want to buy it. He shakes his head no and, looking at the soldiers, murmurs that he "can't." Al-Shabaab, it appears, is less gone than we're being told, and when night comes, they'll return to tax the old man of the sea. A third unit made up of Bancroft men escorts Fatima, the nurse who has accompanied us from Mogadishu, to the dry stone dispensary where a hundred or so women clad in brightly colored dresses wait, as on the day of the burial. They tell us of their successive pregnancies; their violent husbands; the malnourished, coughing child who has stopped growing. The worrisome sign is that the men aren't showing themselves. Except one, about fifty, with a Salafi beard, who appears as balloons are being handed out to the children. "You don't belong here!" he screams with overplayed anger. "It's my job to pass out the balloons!" A French soldier from Bancroft, his face hidden behind a scarf, leads us back to the vehicles. Message received. Time to break camp.

At breakfast, the officers in our compound, accustomed as they are to "Mogadishu music," don't seem all that surprised by the sound of an explosion. According to military radio, it's a suicide car, the third in the past month in the area known as Kilometer 4, the giant traffic circle near Bakara Market that is the heart of the city. At the wheel was a female member of the Somali diaspora who, according to a cousin, had returned to the country after studying in London and had her brain washed by Bollywood-style movies describing the paradise in which her lost loved ones were waiting for her. In the time it takes us to get there (an hour at most), everything has been cleared away. Not a trace of the demolished car. In a city where you have to be very highly placed to get an ambulance, the bodies of the victims (five? six? more? no one knows) have been evacuated. It's possible to discern, while weaving through the sea of cars and *tuk-tuks* that have resumed their endless rondo and absurd concert of horns, dark traces of dried blood that weren't thoroughly scrubbed from the asphalt. Life reasserts its rights. The cannibal city, devouring the dead and the living alike, returns to its comatose panting. Nothing happened in Mogadishu. And our fixer seems to be the only one who remembers that it is often just at these moments, when the traffic resumes, when the traffic jams are at their peak, that al-Shabaab sends in a second car bomb that, with everyone now packed in, will cause fifty deaths.

Basically, there are only two forces that can impose any semblance of order on the insane chaos. First, the Turks. There was a time when the Arabs were also here. Arabs from the Emirates, to be specific. But one day, when their plane touched down with ten million in cash intended for Somali soldiers, overzealous customs inspectors confiscated the suitcases, so they got angry and pulled out. And with the Americans limiting themselves to air strikes, the European Union administering a massive aid program of which no trace can be detected on the ground, and the Chinese not yet aware of the interest of this accursed country, only the Turks remain, and they are only too happy to find themselves alone on the Horn of Africa, adjacent to Djibouti, facing eminently strategic Yemen. And as usual, the Turks play a double game. On the one hand, a spanking-new embassy – standing, not leveled; plus a colossal military base from which they never emerge; Recep Tayyip Erdoğan's name is plastered in roman and Arabic characters all along the main arteries. And when, on December 28, on the route inland to Afgoye, it's their turn to fall victim to a suicide truck, they raise the tone and pretend to support "the legitimate government of President Farmaajo." But on the other hand, there is the Turks' complacency toward al-Shabaab fundamentalism, which is not far from the ideology of the Muslim Brotherhood; there is their refusal to join Operation Atalanta, launched by the Europeans to fight the piracy that funds many of the attacks; and there is their determination to close their eyes to the fact that it is through a Turkish black market that Somali soldiers sell the jihadists weapons and ammunition paid for with international aid.

The second of the two forces is Bancroft. Yes, the same Bancroft that, upon our arrival, I took for just an NGO tasked with housing the African Union. In an earlier life, Bancroft's boss, Richard Rouget, was a French lieutenant in Bob Denard's crew of "Horribles." And in an even earlier life, he was one of the far-right militants with whom young people of my stripe clashed in Paris's Latin Quarter. But now he's an archly novelistic character, closer to "the man who would be king" than to the standard mercenary, just as capable of reciting, at the evening barbecue, a verse from Baudelaire as a page from John le Carré. Although he plays a dandy who never carries a weapon (because "when it goes down there will always be enough around to pick up"), he has put together a strange foreign legion made up of eighteen nationalities. I discover that in one operation after another its members are doing a lot more than "mentoring" Africans. There's Sigitas, a Lithuanian, whose job it is to disarm sophisticated explosives. There's Dariusz, the Pole, who, in his daily briefing, with the instinct of an old fox of urban guerrilla warfare, points on the satellite map to the checkpoint through which the next truckload of charcoal laced with explosives will pass. There's Ingemar, the Swedish medic, who is always first to arrive at the site of a killing. And there's Rouget himself, who, when the Ugandans forget that there are treacherous anti-tank trenches dug under the asphalt of the Lido, assembles foot soldiers, leads the assault, and takes a round in the thigh. Incredible but true. This Mad Max outlaw city—whose army is torn into rival factions, whose AMISOM-allied contingents think of little else but going home, and whose intelligence service is rife with Qataris if not with al-Shabaab operatives—has placed its fate in the hands of a hundred private soldiers who seem to stem from a Joseph Conrad novel.

And then there's the mayor. He's an ex-warlord. Not an al-Shabaab fundamentalist—a warlord. And the head of a clan. Which is to say, in Somali political terms, a sworn enemy of al-Shabaab. I have an image of him perched on a mountain of rubble after an explosion—he cuts a fine figure. But what is the legitimacy of a mayor appointed by a president who is holed up in his own palace? And how do you govern when your predecessor died in a suicide attack in the middle of a city council meeting? Because it's late at night, he receives us at his home, a villa at the end of a street strewn with garbage, no electricity, patrolled by a praetorian guard busy chewing their ration of *khat*. He seems distracted, bothered by the burden of having to respond to my questions. Seated on a raised throne replete with gilt, never raising his eyes from his phone, he lightens up only to discuss the thorny question of whether his surname (everyone in Somalia has one) is "Finish," because his principle has always been to take no prisoners and instead to finish off his wounded adversaries, or "Filish," like the dance of the same name, of which he improvises an entrechat, barefoot, on his toes, knees half bent in his metallic pants. This he does very smoothly, a mixture of Pink Panther and Moonwalk. And as for his city, he agrees to talk about it only later on, during dinner, when I raise the idea of an international conference on battered, urbicidal cities, to which Mogadishu would be invited. "I'll organize it!" he shouts, without ceasing to chew his meat. And when I observe that organizing such an event and bringing in representatives from Kabul, Beirut, Vukovar, and Sarajevo would require an enormous amount of infrastructure, he screams at his terrified assistants, who are feverishly taking notes: "Infrastructure! Infrastructure! Like for the Olympics, I can and I will organize the infrastructure!"

To experience an attempted stoning, complete with a screaming crowd throwing real stones, I had to wait for Mogadishu. We had been directed to one of the infamous tunnels stinking of dead rats that the al-Shabaab extremists still use to move from house to house. We passed through the Corniche, which, with its villas perched over the sea and its blind windows exposed to ships' cannons, gave me the impression of a Tangiers studded, every fifty meters or so, with testimonials to battles and massacres. With a fixer but no other escort, we entered one of those mazes of crumbled stone, of balconies hanging in empty space, of riads gone to seed – places foreigners never go. A few minutes further on, we fall upon a group of young people in jeans sitting on the ground against a wall, dazed by the early afternoon heat. One of them, perhaps the leader of the pack, gets up and shouts at us, his speech slurred from drugs, that he doesn't want to be photographed. Another chimes in that they don't want any foreigners here – no infidels, no Yankees. And as we try awkwardly to negotiate and to assure them that we aren't Yankees, that we respect Somalia, and that we are friends of the Sufi Islam that is the pride of their country, they become even angrier and begin pitching things at us – an empty Coke bottle, a shard of glass, a hail of stones. We owe our safety to the driver of the armored personnel carrier who, when we didn't return, set out to find us. Weapon in hand, with a cool all the more remarkable because AMISOM rules prohibit him from firing his gun, he calms the kids down.

And the members of al-Shabaab in all this? I'll describe one. For his safety, let's call him Ahmed. He's a European freight forwarder who organized our meeting in the port in the trailer of an abandoned truck at the end of one of those lines of multicolored containers that form veritable streets he knows like the back of his hand. It was his job, he explains, to keep an eye on the containers, right? To collect taxes from their owners? And didn't he get so good at it that he didn't even make the owners open them before levying the tax? Yes, but that's when his troubles began. The Amniyat, the shadowy al-Shabaab intelligence service that is, with its hundreds of overpaid informants, the elite of this army of barbarians, concluded that he was lenient. They didn't like it when he asked to be transferred to the coast guard – to chase pirates instead. Suspecting him of trafficking with the Burundis, they started spying on him, calling his kids at night to scare them, summoning him for no reason, as on the morning toward the end of 2018 when he was called to a village thirty kilometers from the city (a three-day drive) to take part in a session of serial decapitations. And then, one day, a step too far: he was ordered to organize an attack in his own neighborhood on a businessman who wouldn't cough up protection money but who belonged to Ahmed's own clan. This he could not do. Is there a limit to a man's madness? A line that can't be crossed? That one thing to make him jump ship? How many Ahmeds have escaped this mafia, even if it meant living in fear, scuttling from hideout to hideout in hopes of being recruited by a foreign outfit? Few, I fear, very few. And I reach the end of this investigation with the feeling that, after twenty years of futile war, al-Shabaab still reigns over Somalia.

10

RETURN TO BANGLADESH

Bangladesh, March 2020

A fanfare of flutes and drums. A line of waiflike children clapping in rhythm. Former fighters with white beards singing in unison the anthem of free Bengal. And, stretched between bamboo poles, yellow banners proclaiming: "Welcome Back to Jessore, Bernard-Henri Lévy!" Yes, Jessore. It was almost fifty years ago. In 1971, with a handful of others, I had answered André Malraux's call to French youth for the formation of an international brigade similar to that of the Spanish civil war, this time to oppose the horrible crimes of the Pakistani army in what was still East Pakistan. I had landed in Calcutta. Crossed the Indian border in Satkhira with a topaz dealer who had fled his village but was coming back for his three daughters. And I had ended up right here, seventy kilometers to the north, in Jessore, which was being pounded by bombs and machine-gun fire. It barely qualified as a city at the time. The airport wasn't here. Neither was the tangle of colonial-era houses, unfinished new buildings, and mud huts. Nor the population of ragged children, zebu dealers, and discouraged beggars intrigued by this foreigner moved to tears by the festival in his honor. But there is the same pale sky. The same tangy fragrance commingled with pungent whiffs of cooked coconut oil. And, immediately upon leaving the bazaar, on both sides of a badly built road bearing a mad competition of rickshaws, wagons of firewood, and busses packed to the roof (which, with every curve, seemed on the point of toppling), the same bleak plain of rice paddies. The Bangladesh of my twenties.

Akim Mukherjee was the young Maoist leader who had picked me up in Satkhira, behind the front line, after I parted ways with the topaz dealer. A half century later, I gave his name to Mofidul Hoque of the Liberation War Museum in Dhaka. He passed it along to the police who, because the underground communists of the time went by a dizzying number of noms de guerre, had some trouble finding him. But now here we are at this village house overlooking a pond where Akim and I had spent a few nights before taking off over the marshes of rice and blood in search of Marxist-Leninist brochures, of which Bangladesh was a major producer and which I would work into *Les Indes Rouges,* my first book.

The man of about fifty who is waiting for me at the door of the house intones, "My father is dead," before introducing himself as my friend's son. "He often spoke of you," he continues as we move out onto the veranda, where dishes of banana await us. "A young Frenchman with a yellow jacket . . . He saved this . . . " From a plastic sleeve full of yellowed press clippings he pulls a business card printed with the address of the École Normale Supérieure on the Rue d'Ulm, onto which I had scrawled my parents' address. "But come see your room. It's the room in which he died. Nothing has been moved." I am not sure if I recognize the webbed bed. Or the table on which stand old collections of Bengali poetry. But what is definitely the same is this: on the floor against the wall, near a small altar bearing vials of incense, candles, multicolored devotional images, and holy bells, are two faded black-and-white portraits of Marx and Lenin, worshipped on par with Shiva and Vishnu. As I move to open the shutter and let in some light, I jostle the photos. From behind these relics of a world that had aimed to become the entire human race scuttles an immense black spider, which settles on a lantern. A sign. But of what?

I meet Saleha Begum and Rezia Begum Kamla at the Liberation War Museum. They are *birangona*—which literally means national heroines. And they owe that status to the fact that during the war they and four hundred thousand other women were raped by the rabble of the Pakistan Armed Forces. When the natural consequences of those attacks arrived nine months later, in the weeks surrounding the proclamation of independence, President Mujibur Rahman made a historic decision. Instead of shunning or ostracizing them, as would have occurred in most traditional societies, Rahman, the father of the nation, embraced the victims as if they were his own daughters. Do the women know that for several months I had been acting as a sort of intellectual mercenary, placing in the service of the new state the scraps of economics that I had absorbed from the books of Charles Bettelheim, an expert on Chinese people's communes and a friend of Louis Althusser? And were they told that, when I had the privilege of meeting the new president, I was among those who suggested to him that their suffering, their innocence, but also their resilience made them natural heroines in the nascent national story, and that they should be formally acknowledged as such? Yes, they had heard about that. But what they were most acutely aware of was the ongoing revolution in the West to criminalize violence against women. These ladies are very old indeed. They take small steps. Some of their peers, clad in brightly colored saris and wearing their finest nose pins, arrived at the event in wheelchairs. But what fierce determination to right past wrongs! What passion in their accounts of the years of struggle it took them to win the status not just of victims but of Mukti Bahini, full-fledged freedom fighters. And with what youthful joy do they declare themselves, from their wheelchairs, the vanguard of world feminism!

Sheikh Hasina is the daughter of Mujibur Rahman. For eleven years she has been the country's prime minister. She is a member of my generation. She knows my story. And that is why she invited me to the ceremonies marking the hundredth anniversary of her father's birth and the fiftieth of the birth of her nation. Because of COVID-19, the festivities are postponed. But I bring her a letter from my own president, Emmanuel Macron, which, again because of the coronavirus and social-distancing rules, I must place on the tea table separating us, just below the portrait of Mujibur Rahman hanging in the simple reception room in which she has received me. She reaches out to take it. Reconsiders. Gives me a complicit smile when her duly-gloved chief of protocol rises to open the letter for her. She has the reputation of being an authoritarian leader, implacable with opponents. Indeed, dressed in her bronze sari, which could be mistaken for armor, her tortoiseshell glasses reflecting the icy gleam of her green eyes, her strong jaw, she has the appearance of Indira Gandhi at the height of her power. But what wins out for the moment is the youthfulness of her expression. Her playful gaiety as we recall shared memories of the successful struggle for national liberation. Her way of feigning surprise when I tell her about the difficulty the police had in tracking Akim Mukherjee, in whose company I experienced, so many years ago, my baptism of fire. And, by contrast, her display of ferocity when I bring up the assassination of her father four years later, in 1975, in a military coup. The whole family fell victim; only she and her younger sister escaped, by virtue of being out of the country at the time. But for these Antigones of Dhaka, no time has elapsed; the desire for vengeance is intact.

In Golora, a suburb of Manikganj, the other Bangladesh begins. The Bangladesh of rural villages. The Bangladesh to which I came, once upon a time, in the company of Rafiq Hussain, the eldest son of the first family I lived with in Dhaka after the liberation. My purpose then was to interview Maulana Bashani, the old Maoist peasant leader who vied with Mujibur Rahman for leadership of the Awami League. A half century later, I am gathering my thoughts before a humble monument, just a small mound of dry stones surrounded by a simple brick wall, under which lie the remains of an unknown number of civilians executed in the final hours of the war. How many mausoleums of this sort does the country hold? How many ossuaries in how many villages, at the end of dirt roads passable only by motorbikes, in the middle of fields of flowers, in the shade of stands of banyan trees? No one knows. The simple fact is that no one knows exactly how many died in this genocide. That it was a genocide – that much is known. According to researchers, the intention was there. There was the systematic nature of the killing. And all the other criteria. But whether it claimed one, two, three, or perhaps four million victims, no one can say. "You are the only people in the world," I tell a group of teenagers who have been following me from Golora and the ruins of its ghost palace, whose facade, with its stairways, draws tourists from Dhaka, "never to be allowed to count its martyrs. You are unique in honoring dead who are not only without graves, but also without number and even without name. In every Bengali village, the work of remembering must continue for as long as witnesses remain in this world. Everywhere, survivors and their descendants must ensure that family stories are told and retold. A great people cannot live with such a massive gap in its memory."

I call her Benazir. We made contact through Facebook. She directs a girls' school in Rajshahi, in the east of the country. She has lived under police protection since she banned the wearing of veils in class. "We need to see our pupils' faces," she begins, sitting with me in the tiny restaurant in old Dhaka, hardly more than a stall, which she picked because they serve *paturi,* thin slices of fish marinated in mustard and wrapped in banana leaves, which was one of my favorite meals during my time there. Then in a quieter voice, after a glance at the neighboring tables, which are too close for comfort, and another at the street, which, at this hour, is so packed with the chaos of scooters, tuk-tuks, and vans driving in every direction that if a terrorist attack were to occur it is a sure bet that no help would get through: "And what's more we're not a madrassa; we have Hindu girls, Buddhists, a few Christians, Shiites. You say Shiites are Muslims? Okay, that's true, but they're in the crosshairs of the Jamiat, that Islamist party the government outlawed because it was serving as a conveyor belt for ISIS . . . " We forget that aspect of things when we talk about Bangladesh. I am not at all sure that, at the time, I was myself aware of this basic cleft in the war with Pakistan. On the one hand, the "land of the pure" whose DNA was Islamic fundamentalism. On the other, a country that, though majority Muslim, is also multi-faith and respectful of its minorities. It would be good to keep that in mind, now that the war between the two Islams is raging across the planet. Bangladesh has a real role to play in the face-off between enlightened and fanatical Islam.

A camp is a camp, of course. And no one will ever hear me say that there are happy refugees. But as chance would have it, I arrive in Cox's Bazar, the sprawling refugee camp in which, for three years, nine hundred thousand Rohingyas have fled anti-Muslim persecution by Burma's Buddhists and its military junta; I arrive just days after visiting Moria, on the Greek island of Lesbos, the landing point for the Syrians that Erdoğan is pushing toward Europe. And, sad to say, the Europeans do not hold the advantage. It is here in the thirty-four camps in Cox's Bazar that NGOs operate more freely. Here that one finds adequate supplies of soap, towels, toothbrushes, and water dispensers. Here that after the initial few weeks of chaos, as survivors of the massacres stripped the hills of wood in an effort to warm themselves, great bamboo walkways were built to connect the parts of what has almost become a city. Here that more than a semblance of a life has been established—with paved paths, clean huts, and even tiny kitchen gardens that enable families to pursue the subsistence agriculture they practiced at home in Burma. To be sure, as in Lesbos, there is friction with adjacent villages that complain about "native Bengalis" being less well off than the newcomers. But the authorities have not buckled. A lesson in the courage of the Rohingya, who have lost everything but their dignity. A lesson, too, in the humanity of the Bengalis, who have nothing but still find the wherewithal to share that nothing with the nine hundred thousand residents of a living purgatory.

I have said nothing of Bangladesh's poverty. Had I forgotten the sweatshops to which the West subcontracts the jobs it no longer wants to grandchildren of the Mukti Bahini hardly older than twelve? Had I forgotten the hordes of unemployed people who contend with stray dogs and rodents for bits of food in the Bashantek dumps in the heart of Dhaka? And had I forgotten that a scene like the following was possible? Still in the middle of Dhaka, the Rupnagar slum burned yesterday down to its pilings. The pestilential cesspool of black water over which the lakeside favela was built is now in the open air. And there, enveloped in an evening mist (though it is high noon), amid the waste, the cracked sewer pipes, the dead rats, and the smoldering bamboo, a man with the eyes of an ascetic, clad in loincloth and mobcap, appears to be doing his ablutions. But no, he is diving repeatedly into the fetid water and dredging it for bits of steel and iron that he will sell for a few takas at the Kawran Bazar flea market . . .

Had I forgotten? No, not exactly. I have not *forgotten* anything. Because, in my day, none of that existed. The Buriganga, which has become a monstrous Alpheus River whose flow is slowed by pileups of plastic, was a real river. The Hazaribagh section of the city, where two hundred thousand people drink, fish, and wade on the banks of a marsh made up of detritus and toxic materials, was a semirural suburb where a guild of tanners practiced their thousand-year-old craft. And the ancestors of my cycle-rickshaw driver were Mukti Bahini who felt no shame about their profession.

Another thing not discussed then but now painfully obvious is that if there is one spot in the world threatened by the coming climate catastrophe, it is right here. Bangladesh is a delta nation. It is a land of seven hundred rivers, some of which, like the Ganges and the Brahmaputra, originate deep in the subcontinent and meet here in order to throw themselves into the Gulf of Bengal. It is the spill point of the torrents formed by melting Himalayan ice; in the season of cyclones and heavy monsoons, those torrents raise river levels and trigger landslides of colossal proportions. The archipelago that I remember lying off the shore of Cox's Bazar is gone. The square islands farther north, with their stunted vegetation, which I do not remember from before: they are all that remains of a former rice paddy. The herring fisherman, only thirty but looking twice as old, has been forced to move his home three times as the sea has devoured his land. The farmer who has never heard of climate change tells me that a new law in Bangladesh has made rivers living beings that must be respected but also tamed. And those fishing boats seen from the Chittagong road being loaded with nets, barrels of brine, and spare masts: why the strange shape, with the bow and the stern curved up and in like a basket or crescent moon? Is it to raise the bow and make it easier for the boat to clear the sandbars that mark where the land once was? Is it to defy the rising sea? To facilitate fishing in shallow water? Or is it to appease the monster in this country where, contrary to the poet's dictum, it is not the desert that grows but the sea? I do not know.

And finally, poor, poor Bangladesh, the front line of the planetary war against radical Islam, poverty, migratory chaos, and ecological cataclysm, has yet another battle to fight—that of the ensuing global pandemic. As if all the others were not enough, Bangladesh has always been a land of fever, diarrhea, respiratory ailments, and skin diseases traceable to the destruction of air and soil. Endemic in the country are lymphatic filariasis, visceral leishmaniasis, melioidosis, fluke worm, dengue fever, and Japanese encephalitis, as well as Nipah and Hendra, those viruses spread from bat droppings that, when transmitted to humans, are fatal in three out of four cases. And I learned at my own expense that the country's water, unless boiled, delivers a variety of malaria that left me flat on my back for days at a stretch. In the midst of which the coronavirus rears its ugly head, first in China, then in Europe and the United States. And this little nation of 160 million people, which, at the time of this writing, in March 2020, had only forty-eight cases and five deaths, is taking up the wartime rhetoric of the West and making the hunt for the "invisible enemy" an absolute priority. Cancellation of the centennial celebration. The appearance, in the streets, of homemade masks in all colors and shapes: beaks of birds, muzzles of animals. And a quarantine that is closing the country's land and air borders at the risk of plunging it deeper than ever into the darkness of solitude and poverty. Is the move a precaution against a disease that, were it to break out in densely populated cities and camps, would cause hundreds of thousands of deaths? Is it the odd revenge of a people defending itself against a plague that, for once, has come from outside, a people possibly harboring the illusion that, in mounting its defense, it is joining the virtuous cycle toward the global health state now under construction? I do not know that, either. Decades ago, I was one of the first to take up the cause of this cursed and splendid country. Fifty years later, I am taking the last flight out for Europe. For the time being, I can only hope and pray.

11

THE DEVIL MADE A STOP AT LESBOS

Lesbos, May 2020

"They didn't even give me a sheet; I delivered the baby without anything, on the plastic floor of my tent; I bled . . . " Who are *they?* Are they the Greek government officials, barricaded within their barbed wire–fenced compound? Are they the NGOs that, in what is called the wild part of the camp, the part that extends along and climbs into the hills of olive trees, are stuck with all the world's misery, coping with neofascists who dream of chasing them off the island, and not knowing which way to turn? Or are they her Afghan tent mates who, because she is Sudanese, didn't respond to her cries for help? The fact is that Fatimah is now on her own in a shelter of white plastic tarps. Her six-month-old baby, carried on her back, is wrapped in a worn T-shirt saying "Welcome to Lesbos" that she has refashioned into a onesie. Her older children, aged eight and two, cling to her, appearing even more scared than she is by the presence of a photographer and an interpreter. In bad Arabic, uttered piecemeal and interspersed with long silences, she offers up the details of her terrifying exodus. The transit camp in Gaziantiep

. . . The husband whom the Greeks sent back to Turkey three days after their arrival, obliging them to pay the Zodiac fare a second time . . . Her admission in extremis because she was pregnant . . . The baby whom the Greek civil authorities did not register and who therefore does not exist . . . It's cold now at the end of May 2020. The rain, which comes in gusts and bursts, seeps through the badly joined pieces of the tent. A smell of humidity, unwashed bodies, and dirty water mingles with that of the vegetable stew simmering near the entrance to the tent. The eight-year-old gets up to stir the pot. A rat scampers between his legs and disappears, without the boy seeming to notice. We are in the Moria camp on Lesbos, one of Greece's most beautiful islands, a place full of history and legend—and, today, Europe's capital of pain.

On my previous visit several months earlier, I had been struck by a report from Doctors without Borders asserting that one of Moria's distinguishing characteristics is child suicide. Here's the story of one child. The boy is twelve. We are within the confines of the camp, in the wild area known as the jungle, where some of the Syrians with whom Erdoğan threatened to inundate Europe last March washed up. For the duration of our interview, except for brief glances at the uncle who saved him and who, as a former teacher in Idlib, is telling his nephew's story for him, the boy keeps his eyes on the ground. It all started, his uncle says, with his nephew's inability to comprehend this new life devoid of prospects. What are we doing here? the child wanted to know. Why can't we go look at the sea, when it's so close? Even when the bombs were falling on Idlib, you would take me to school—so why now do we have to spend entire days doing nothing but stare at the Turkish coast? Are we going to be prisoners here forever? Little by little, the boy stopped talking.

He stopped playing. He spent his days lying in the broken armchair that sits in the middle of the hut and in which I sat before I knew the whole story. He lost interest in his soccer friends. Wouldn't eat and couldn't sleep. Later I learned that one morning, when his uncle was out standing in line to collect their daily ration of bread, a neighbor saw blood flowing in the drainage channel. He rushed in. The boy had traded a box of humanitarian-donated cookies, accumulated one by one during the week, for the razor blades he had used to slash his wrists. I have seen many camps in my life. But rarely the boundless sadness on display here.

At Moria, water is the tragedy. The island, as I've said, is resplendent. Green. Blessed by the gods and by rain. But across the camp's accursed acres, there is no running water. No wells, either. No cisterns that I could see. Just a few showers. At most twenty water stations, where people line up all day to fill their plastic bottles. One per person per day, a representative of the Afghan community tells me. Just one. As incredible as it may seem, nineteen thousand refugees have a single liter of water each day with which to slake their thirst, cook, bathe, do their laundry, and disinfect. And some days, when the water is cut off, they don't have even that and must ration the precious drops that remain to them until the next day. I ask people to talk about it. I ask for confirmation from the head of the Hazara community who, with his wife and two children, occupies the next tent and shows me, as if it were an exhibit to be introduced in evidence, four bottles neatly arranged and already, at mid-morning, half empty. In order to see for myself, I go to the nearest water station, which is in a clearing atop the ruins of some demolished huts. Fifty-odd women are lined up in single file. And, in fact, I see no jerricans. Each woman clutches her plastic bottle. Sometimes two or three bottles, if they are part of a family and can prove it. "You seem surprised," a young Algerian woman says to me in perfect French. She has been waiting for papers for thirteen months. "I'm a philosopher, too," she says. "I admire Camus and Kamel Daoud. And I have a message for you: Look around. Water's not the only thing we lack; we don't have soap, either."

But the worst are the latrines. Because what do you do when an old camp designed for eight hundred soldiers, and then repurposed for three thousand refugees, becomes home to nearly twenty thousand? If a tent stands far enough away from others, a family can dig its own pit into the ground behind the tent. Otherwise there are the convenience tents into which people go one by one to crouch over a plank with a hole in it, placed over a ditch unconnected to any waste-removal system. And finally there are the public (I was going to say "official") latrines installed either by the local administration or by NGOs. These facilities provide a focal point for the anger of these people, deprived of the least shred of privacy. Midway up what passes for a road running along the barbed wire that divides the original camp from its wild extension, one finds a collection of giant, construction-site porta-potties with the flushers out of commission and most of the doors too damaged to close. I go into one. Bowls spattered with excrement. Pits obviously clogged and infested with flies. A fetid odor that stays with me into the vacant lot farther up the road, where I go to kick the ball around with a group of kids, just to get my mind off the latrines. And the *lines*, the eternal lines, implying that there is nothing better to do at Moria than to line up, line up again, and then line up some more. There are those who get impatient, who shove, who urge people to hurry up. There are those who line up only as a precaution, with no pressing need, because, with time at a standstill, the only pastime is to line up for everything and nothing, all blessed day, until you go crazy. Humiliation. Torture. As the rest of Europe is obsessing over public health and hygiene and how often we wash our hands, Moria is beset with infection, corruption, and stench, with little water to be found. *Anus mundi.*

The one miracle, in this context, is that there is not more violence and murder. It is said that when night falls and the police have gone back to their quarters there are fights between Sudanese and Syrians, Afghans and Iranians, Afghans and Afghans – and of all against the handful of Congolese, some Muslim, some Christian, but universally viewed as the damnedest of the damned. I heard – without being able to verify the story – about an adolescent who was knifed for his cell phone the week before we arrived. There is the story of a Pashtun man who allegedly assaulted a Panjshiri woman, during Ramadan no less. I heard about the manhunt that night. The knife wound to the foot. Gangrene. Coma. And a few days later, death, both for lack of early care and because, with the camp quarantined on account of COVID-19, he was taken only very belatedly to the hospital in Mytilene. And then there are the two young women who, although housed in Area C, the supposedly secure part of the camp reserved for orphaned and adolescent girls, tell me that they won't drink a drop of water after 5:00 in the afternoon for fear of having to make their way out to the toilet at night. But the truly extraordinary thing is that this jungle is not more of a jungle than it is. That it is not the site of a full-blown war of all against all. That, despite the deprivation, despite the fear, despite the feeling of having been abandoned by the gods, the Greeks, and the world, despite the supremely sad graffiti the likes of "We are not animals" and

"Europe, why have you abandoned us?" there persists, among these sisters and brothers whom nothing and no one have succeeded in dehumanizing, acts of solidarity that allow life to continue.

We are in the central part of the camp, made up of permanent structures in which immigration officers sit at their stations and the masters of this penal farce apply subtly cruel criteria to make distinctions among degrees of woe: at the bottom of the scale, the much-feared red stamp, which means an indefinite wait at Moria; at the top are the rare and magical blue seals that confer the right to migrate to the continent; between the two is the black seal accorded to minors and the incurably ill, known as the "vulnerable," who may, one day, depending on the efforts of highly paid lawyers knowledgeable in the mysteries of the local administration, gain the right to pass out of limbo and leap from black to blue.

The director of the camp ventures out to show us what he calls the women's neighborhood, located behind the warehouses. It is a fenced, half-covered promenade onto which small dormitories open. And suddenly the promenade is full of angry women, most of them African, clad in stretch pants and bodysuits, fists raised, shouting. "They're doing that for you," grumbles the director. "They don't want you to take their picture." Except the opposite is true. They motion for us to come closer. And, like sublime harpies, storm goddesses right out of Homer and Hesiod, they begin to chant, "Moria no good! Moria no good!" Panic on the part of the authorities. Camp staff try to push the girls back, causing them to shout even louder. An anti-riot police unit arrives, which I manage to persuade to fall back with me. Who are these women? Why are they in this reserved area? Are they really, as the staff tries to tell me, "unmarried women" who need to be "protected"? I don't get a convincing answer. Regretfully, I move away. And for what seems like a long time, I hear in the distance the inspiring clamor of the rebels of Moria.

I brought masks from Paris. Notebooks, too, of course. Packets of pain relievers. But mostly, probably out of conformism and in deference to the spirit of the moment, and because I believed that COVID-19 would, even here, seem like the apocalypse, boxes of beautiful blue masks, new and pristine. Word gets around. Gaggles of little kids are ogling the red suitcase that I left with the aid workers. And when I go to collect it to take it up to the clearing where two former Syrian White Helmets, now converted into justices of the peace, recommended that I give them out, yet another riot awaits us. The notebooks are received with relative calm. The medications as well. But when the time comes to open the treasure chest containing the thousand masks, the crowd becomes a crush. A stampede, insanity. The excitement is about to turn into a brawl. "Not all at once," screams a White Helmet. "One at a time. And one mask per child, just one; otherwise there won't be enough to go around." But his words only raise the heat. The prize is to the one who can push the hardest, has the sharpest elbows, and can jump the highest, when I, after being shoved and almost knocked over, raise the package over my head and call out for calm. It turns out that this isn't a distribution, it's a party. Better than a party, it's a happening that is both joyful and heartbreaking. Because when I've given the last mask to the last child, the White Helmet comes clean. All the scourges of the world can be found at Moria. Diarrhea. Diphtheria. Rare and unknown diseases. But look, here's how it is, he tells me: no cases of COVID-19 have been recorded. I don't know whether to laugh or cry. I decide to watch as the children put on what now seem like Mardi Gras masks.

I also wanted to see the fascists. I had seen the images of the anti-migrant militants pushing back, with gaff hooks, the boats coming in from Turkey, and I really wanted to know what goes on in someone's head when he does such a thing. Well, I didn't have to look far. Constantinos Moutzouris, the governor of Lesbos, organized the meeting in the paneled, bronze-appointed room in which I assume the island's municipal council meets. You have to imagine the boogaloo boys and self-appointed militiamen in the Senate chamber at the Capitol. (A note: As I reread my words prior to publication, in the last stages of editing, this sentence sits eerily, knowing the last revolt of the Proud Boys on that fateful January 6, 2021 . . .) Or a gathering of white supremacists at the UN General Assembly. Because there, quietly seated side by side, each behind his microphone, were twenty local notables, some boatmen or fishermen, others shopkeepers or teachers, all with nothing on their mind except migrants. It was a free-for-all in which nothing was too absurd or off-limits. The forced Islamization of the island. Churches desecrated and defiled. ISIS infiltrators. A plot by George Soros. Wives and daughters who can no longer go out at night because, locked up or not, hordes of foreigners are on the prowl to rape them. And then the clincher: Kostas Alvanopoulos, retired from the hotel business, recounting, as if it were an act of heroism, how he had seen a boat in the bay rescuing shipwreck victims and how, when he realized that the boat was not flying a Greek flag, that the captain was German, and that the coast guard was doing nothing to prevent the "invaders" from landing, he "saw red" and took matters into his own hands by repelling the landing. Is he proud of what he did? Naturally. At the risk of drowning children? Why not? Isn't he one of the 310 so-called defenders of the island who have been prosecuted for endangering the lives of others? Yes, but the purity of the Hellenic race is worth a trial. I felt sick. It was the first time in my life that I had found myself in such a situation. Confronted with such open, proud, and despicable hate. What does one do in the face of such shamelessness? Alas, nothing; one can only hope that justice will be served.

The next day at dawn, we return one last time to the site of comparative humaneness that is the hospice of Moria. To keep hopelessness at bay, I try to focus on some pleasant impressions. The face of Georgia Rasvitsou, a lawyer in Mytilene, who accompanied me on this assignment. With her sylph-like silhouette right out of the romance by Longus, the bard of Lesbos, she is one of the last exemplars of the hospitable and fraternal land that, five years ago (it seems like a century), welcomed in the first life rafts that washed up on the beaches of Skala Sykaminia like so many princesses and princes Europa descended, once upon a time, from their winged bulls. The grace of Jesuit priest Maurice Joyeux, who still hasn't recovered from the arson last March that reduced to ashes the school for migrant children he had run three kilometers south of Moria. With his own hands he has built a new school in the middle of one of the most squalid and sloping parts of the camp, standing on a foundation of pallets and compacted garbage. It is set to open soon. Its classes, offered at three levels, will be like so many virtuous circles in a hell transcended. And yesterday evening, as night fell and the camp was preparing to close over its wounds and its dangers, this poetic apparition: Kokowumba and his trio of golden-voiced migrants, channelers of Fela, Alpha Blondy, and Bob Marley, whom we find among a group of street vendors gathered on the asphalt to trade rolls, sodas, and single cigarettes. Are the singers there for the kids listening in a circle around them? Are they rehearsing a concert for the residents of the camp? Or are they serenading well-meaning French visitors to whom, with smiles on their lips and tears in their eyes, they sing, "Don't cry! Don't cry!"?

When one comes back from that, when one has stared squarely at such a concentration of horror and distress, when, upon return, one is haunted by images of scabrous children, of women with their feet bare and their innocence trampled, one cannot avoid a certain question that sweeps away all of the ideological and political quarrels: "What should we do?" Offer aid, of course. Tell the story. Relay, as best one can, the words of the afflicted. But the disaster of Moria is such that there really is only one response. Close it. Bulldoze it. Or preserve it, if you will, but preserve it as you might preserve a memorial of inhumanity and shame. There is no way to *repair* hell. Which means that the women, the men, the children languishing in this open-air prison for the sole crime of having dreamed of Europe must absolutely and unconditionally be welcomed among us. Welcomed into Greece, for a start, but also into the rest of our old continent, which now has a choice between losing its honor or gaining from the souls waiting on our doorstep. A wake-up call to Kyriakos Mitsotakis. To Angela Merkel, Emmanuel Macron, and all the rest. A humble petition to statesmen and stateswomen who, confronted with the abomination of this human landfill that we have allowed to fester, no longer have the right to bog down in interminable discussions of immigration loopholes, immigration quotas, good immigration, bad immigration, or migratory policy in general. In the face of the emergency that is Moria and of the symbol of these pilgrims treated like lepers on the very spot where Europa and Zeus invented the European pilgrimage, they have no choice but to wash the stain from the gold-starred flag and to make an exception. Do the math. Run the numbers. Five hundred million Europeans live in twenty-seven nations, to whom I propose to add nineteen thousand suffering souls. A drop of water in the ocean of our prosperity. The Greeks have a symbol for this: *epsilon.*

12

SORROW AND BROTHERHOOD IN LIBYA

Libya, July 2020

This is no ordinary adventure.

You're bumping along on a bad road in western Libya, between Misrata and Tripoli, where the fighting raged a few weeks ago during the offensive launched from the east by "Marshal" Khalifa Haftar.

In Tarhouna, you've just toured an immense killing field where the bodies of forty-seven men, women, and children, some with their hands tied behind their back, were exhumed from a mass grave on June 10. The murders are attributed to militia groups that favor the forces in the eastern half of the country.

You double back through an intersection that, an hour earlier, was indistinguishable from all the other intersections everywhere in Libya, with their bare squares and withered palms, their shaky lamp posts against which locals lean to smoke, the shells of cars, stripped clean, abandoned on the sidewalk alongside overflowing garbage cans.

And then suddenly you encounter a group of armed men in

sand-colored uniforms, accompanied by jeering civilians armed with Kalashnikovs, who begin firing and shouting "Jewish dog!" as a pickup truck fitted with one of those 14.5 millimeter anti-aircraft guns that can cut open a tank screeches to a halt in front of your convoy.

Things don't stop there.

You hardly have time to wonder whether your car was hit, whether your photographers, in the car behind you, are all right, or whether the two drivers will know not to stop and, if necessary, to plow on through the barricade when another, lighter pickup gives chase, manages to pass you, and stops in a cloud of dust at the end of the straightaway three hundred yards ahead. The driver flings open both doors, jumps out, Kalashnikov in hand, and takes his turn taking aim at you.

At full speed, you move to the narrow shoulder, skirting a ditch, as your security man, seated next to the driver and screaming, "Don't stop; don't stop!" grabs the AK-47 lying between the two front seats, within reach of both of them. With everyone praying that the fanatic standing on the asphalt doesn't open fire, the GMC carrying your photographers accelerates and passes on the left, tearing off one of the doors of the pursuer's pickup.

To block the pursuers, a third car, an escort provided by the Misrata police upon your arrival, spins around and lets you get by with the grinding of shot brakes and contradictory orders barking from walkie-talkies before coming to a halt athwart the road.

When your license plate shows up on social networks, your driver gets an order to come into an unmarked police station located a few kilometers away behind a high metal wall that seems to be melting in the heat so you can change vehicles.

—

When the plate of this new vehicle, a pickup less conspicuous than the car that you've just hastily abandoned, also appears almost immediately on Facebook and Twitter, you understand from the shouts coming through the walkie-talkies that you've been sold out and are being monitored; that "the traitors" aren't going to let you go; that a "rebel," a "snitch," has given the pack pursuing you the wherewithal to find and stop you; and that you'll have to take another route.

And then here you are, several hours later, at the end of the runway at the Misrata airport, where the plane you came in on awaits, its engines idling in preparation for takeoff.

* * *

What just happened?

By the time I reached charming Tarhouna, it had probably already begun.

The city of Tarhouna and its outskirts are unknown to the world and ignored in most of the reports of wartime Tripolitania, but they hold the dubious distinction of having been for decades under the control of the al-Khani clan, for whom the art of political reversal seems to be both a favored weapon and a governing technique.

"There's not just one mass grave," the young soldier in a desert ranger's uniform told me, once I had gained his confidence. Wearing a bush hat, with his rifle and two ammo belts slung over his shoulders, he guided me in the oppressive heat over a landscape of sand and death. "Here in this first ring you have the ones killed this year, from the war with Haftar, with a little flag to mark certain individuals or groups or the place where the dismembered body of a young woman was found."

"Over there," he continued, pointing at the endless sea of sand, dotted with little piles of rubble and rectangular graves outlined with quicklime, are "the casualties from two years ago," when the militias were fighting each other and "Fathi Bashagha, our current interior minister," hadn't yet "imposed order."

"And then here" – we stepped under a red tape that, as at a crime scene, marks off an area that one is theoretically not supposed to enter – "this is the place where the victims of 2010 were dug up, from when the al-Khanis and their militia, al-Khanya, were working for Qaddafi and doing his dirty work."

I can't see the young man's masked face.

He's wearing an ochre scarf that comes up to his eyes. It is molded so closely to his features that he looks like the Invisible Man wrapped in his bandages.

But from his obviously educated voice (perhaps he is a student or a young volunteer), I sense that the story he tells is a little beyond him, that he doesn't understand the why of this litany of murders, even if, in every case, he knows the precise dates and the sites.

I have seen Libya's martyred cities.

I saw little else during the 2011 war of liberation in which I placed so much hope, when nearly every day brought news of the discovery of a new mass grave.

But cities martyred so many times are no ordinary thing: towns whose vanished citizens pile up like geological strata attesting to a succession of crimes, each of which seems to have been committed to avenge the previous one; necropolises populated by so many dead, whose bodies have been brought to a Tripoli laboratory for DNA identification but for the most part will remain, even if an exam links them with a name, forever without a grave. No, that is no ordinary thing.

Is it because of what I have seen and heard that I suddenly became, for some, an undesirable? These repeated crimes, committed in common, might they be the guilty secret of a city that has not managed to free itself of its executioners, let alone to punish them? Might Tarhouna be a Thebes on Libyan land, whose dead souls haunt not only the city's survivors but also outsiders, like Gilles Hertzog, Marc Roussel, and myself, who try to break the silence? Is that how I ought to have interpreted the nervousness of my fixer when, as the visit wore on, he murmured to me that we should let the dead bury the dead and move on, without delay? Perhaps.

* * *

Before Tarhouna, I was a hundred kilometers to the east, in Al-Khums, the Arab name of Leptis Magna, the largest ancient city on the south shore of the Mediterranean and proof, if proof were needed, that Libya was, before becoming Berber, Arab, and Muslim, a Roman land.

And there, in this magnificent and inspired place where, like it or not, East and West crossed paths, in this ancient melting pot where civilizations succeeded each other without ever completely disappearing or ceasing their secret dialogue of stone, I did something that must have provoked the evil spirits already irritated by my visit to Libya. (Islamic radicals? Diehard Qaddafists? Saif al-Islam, the dictator's son, who I am told still lives in the country, and whom, though he has become a bit mad and spends his nights in a watched house in Zintan singing "Bella Ciao," the Russians and Turks might eventually agree to put in power?)

I wandered through the still-standing porticos of the ancient city.

I passed under the arches built to celebrate victories over the intractable Punic tribes who captured Gustave Flaubert's fancy in *Salammbô*.

I strolled the serpentine pavements, the perfect stones polished by wind and sea seeming like those of a revived city.

I climbed onto the proscenium of the empty theater in the company of a small group of young Libyans who told me how they, their fathers, and the fathers of their fathers defended the site against the wounds of time, earthquakes, pillagers, Qaddafists, and the depredations of the Islamic State, which wanted to destroy Leptis Magna as it had Palmyra.

And, intimidated by the silence, overcome by my audience's emotion and my own, I read out the "Appeal to People of Good Will" that I had first drafted in Paris with a handful of friends from the Libyan revolution orphaned of their dream and living in exile.

> We know, Libyan brothers, that you are at the edge of an abyss and in despair.
>
> Years of civil war, destruction, and fratricidal violence have robbed you of your brothers, your sisters, your children, your parents.
>
> The beautiful plan that we conceived, as Libyans and Europeans working side by side, of a fraternal, democratic Libya free from dictatorship, seems to have vanished in the sand.
>
> Today you are a country divided in two. The idea of the Libyan people has nearly ceased to exist.

So here, from Leptis Magna, I join you in issuing this modest appeal to all who are not resigned to the eternal recurrence of the worst.

For peace, comity, and freedom cannot come from outside; they must come from within.

It is up to Libyans, and Libyans alone, to rid Libya of occupying forces who are present only to bring back a tyrant and to pillage the country.

It is up to Libyans from all sides to reconcile Tripoli, Misrata, Zliten, Benghazi, and Derna, sister cities that can, if you will it, rediscover a common destiny.

Nine years ago, friends came to your aid when you rose up against tyranny. That was a moment of shared greatness.

Others came later, following your war of liberation, to sow discord. And that, in the West and in the East, is the poison that is destroying you today.

Now it is up to you to take the initiative once again.

Up to you to create a third force, a force composed of free citizens, which alone can forgive crimes and bind the wounds of our recent history.

May this appeal, if it reaches beyond these colonnades and flies from ruin to ruin, cross over the border that today separates you from your sisters and brothers in Cyrenaica.

Too much blood has been shed.

Too many mothers, in every town across the country, mourn their lost sons.

Too many young widows have learned that their tears will not bring back a husband killed in fratricidal conflict.

> Libya is big enough, and rich enough, for all her children.
>
> Throughout the world, and particularly in France, you have friends who hope that you will make this leap.

It seems likely now that this strange appeal – which, as I was voicing it, seemed almost surreal – fell into the silence of the ruins.

I'm inclined to think that it was not heard beyond the small circle of those present and that the local station that had organized this little ceremony, upon reflection, decided not to broadcast it, but that enemy ears had gotten wind of it . . .

What is certain is that, after the ambush in Tarhouna, these words are a dead letter.

* * *

Earlier still was my return to Misrata.

Since 2011 I had been wanting to see the city again.

I first visited it on assignment for *Paris Match* in the days following the deaths by mortar fire of Chris Hondros and Tim Hetherington, two worthy successors to the great Robert Capa.

Arriving by sea from Malta on the ship of a privateer who knew how to get around the blockade, I discovered the spirit of resistance of a city as besieged as Sarajevo had been in the mid-1990s.

And there, bowled over by so much bravery, I realized that, with the right arms, the Misrata brigades alone could liberate Tripoli and put an end to a war that might have gone on forever with opponents entrenched on the shores of Sirte and Ras Lanuf.

In Misrata now, I am visited at my hotel by a member of the parliament in Tripoli who tells me how much he misses the time when France stood at the side of all the proponents of free Libya, bar none.

I make the acquaintance of Mohamed Raed, a sort of Libyan Hamdi Ulukaya (Chobani yogurt's Kurdish founder), a manufacturer of dairy products and the incarnation of the spirit of peaceful trade that is the soul of Misrata and which has enabled him, despite the war, not to miss a single day of delivering yogurt to the two Libyas: the one of Marshal Haftar in the east and the other of Prime Minister Fayez al-Sarraj in the west.

I meet representatives of the Misrata youth who, in 2015, alone and without coalition members or international support, retook Sirte and Sabratha from the Islamic State. I listen as they recount the inglorious flight of the terrorist leader responsible for the decapitation, in February of that year, of twenty-one Egyptian Coptic Christians. (They are still pursuing him.) I ask them to tell me about the death in combat, at the gates of Sirte, of Abdel Rahman al-Kissa, the president of the city's bar association who, a few weeks before, had come to Paris to deliver an official invitation for me to return to Misrata, where the city council at the time had made me an honorary citizen—one of the very few honors I have accepted in my lifetime.

I reunite with General Ramadan Zarmuh, whom I had brought to France in mid-siege to secure from President Sarkozy the equipment that his units needed to swoop down on Tripoli. He has aged. The General Patton of 2011 has become a fragile, melancholy Cincinnatus. None of the "national reconciliation committees" that he has been asked to chair, year after year, can substitute for the time when Libyans got along, which now seems so long ago.

Finally I retrace my steps down Tripoli Avenue, which, at the time, with its gutted buildings, incinerated cafés, and minarets blasting recorded airplane noise to make the attackers believe that the allies were approaching, was the very image of devastation. Now, life has returned. The little open-air war museum is now a real museum. The power-generating plant outside the city, the ruins of which we had filmed – the twisted metal, the molten girders, the blistered, crumbling walls, crushed pipes, colossal plates of steel crumpled like paper, cables dangling in empty space like inverted candelabras, and that piece of roof, intact but so darkened by the flame that one might have taken it for a gold frieze on the pediment of one of the temples of Leptis Magna; that same power plant is now operating again as if nothing had happened. Everything, even memories of the horror, seems this morning to have woven a magic spell, as in Baudelaire's "Little Old Women."

My sole regret – though the advice that produced it proved prescient – was to have forgone a pilgrimage to the deserted, silent pier where, after a thirty-six-hour voyage with no navigational instruments or landmarks, we had waited for the city authorities. Now, I'm told, that's where "the Turks" operate night and day in defiance of the embargo, unloading their illegal cargo.

* * *

I believe, now, that the reason lies there.

Contrary to what I've read since the Tarhouna ambush from many conspiracists writing from both the northern and southern rims of the Mediterranean, I entered Libya with a valid visa, duly issued.

I was no one's guest and had no intention of immersing myself in disputes between opposing factions, between Tripolitania and Cyrenaica, disputes that are infinitely less important in my eyes than the urgency of seeing Libya's civil society finally take its destiny into its own hands.

I had no other agenda but to reconnect with a people to whom I have given so much of myself, to sound an appeal, in Leptis Magna and elsewhere, for unity and peace, and to bring back from my trip the report you are reading here.

And yet I may have had something else in the back of my mind. That is the mistake we are making by leaving the field open, in Libya as elsewhere, to Turkey and its Islamo-fascist ambitions.

The urgency of seeing France adjust its position in one of those civil wars where one is always wrong to desert, yes, but just as wrong to choose plague over cholera.

And the need, if the adjustment didn't happen, to ensure that at least one French voice would be there to proclaim, from the land that France helped to liberate, words of fraternity and healing.

I knew all too well that this idea would displease the local janissaries of Sultan Erdoğan, who did me the dubious honor, at the moment of the fall of the Muslim Brotherhood in Egypt in 2013 and the coup by Abdel Fattah el-Sisi, of publicly naming me as one of those responsible for the event.

But what I did not imagine, given my enthusiasm for the trip and possibly my naïveté, was the infernal machine that had been set in motion as soon as I informed Tripoli's interior ministry of my reporting plans.

The minister, Fathi Bashagha, by virtue of being the country's top cop, is the regime's strongman. And he is also one of the few who have expressed the desire to see Paris offer a counterweight to Ankara. Yet he must defer to the incumbent prime minister, al-Sarraj, who is a puppet of the Turks.

As soon as he's informed of my visit, al-Sarraj arranges an initial leak to an Algerian rag that runs a headline about the "criminal

Zionist returning to the scene of his crime." And then another notice, appearing on Turkish and Qatari Facebook pages, offers the details of the more or less fake itinerary that I had been required to provide.

I marvel at the hysteria of the social networks that present me sometimes as an emissary of France and the accomplice of its allegedly unnuanced commitment to Haftar's forces; at other times as a provocateur and a warmonger who has come to assist in the dismantling of a great Arab country; and at still other times (hey, lies are cheap) as a double agent secretly working for the Muslim Brotherhood.

The result is that I may have had pinned on my back a target representing a settling of accounts between those who, like Fathi Bashagha, say they believe in government's duty to ensure, among other things, the security of a foreign journalist, and those, like al-Sarraj, who profess no such belief; between those who, like the former, wish to bring the militias to heel and replace them with a sovereign force, and those who, because they derive power and profit from the maintenance of the militias, do not wish to dismantle them; in short, exactly as in Cyrenaica, a struggle between those who seek new avenues of negotiation and new peace talks and those who will spare nothing, up to and including the last Libyan life, to allow the country to continue to serve as a battlefield for the murderous rivalry between the renascent Ottoman and Russian Empires.

Beloved and afflicted Libya.

Site of a moment of greatness where nine years ago Western powers for the first time showed that they were not forever fated to blindly and eternally support tyrants against their own people.

It was to mark and celebrate that unprecedented event that I returned.

And it is in the hope of seeing that event repeated that I will go back again – next time to Benghazi and Derna.

For the moment, I offer these impressions of a Libya once more martyred, under the boot, but not purged of the intoxicating taste of freedom.

I offer this account seen and heard from free Libyans who have not renounced their oath, like the one sworn in Tobruk, to persist until a civil and democratic government has been established across the entire country.

Libya is at a crossroads. As are we. But let us take note. Here, on Libya's shores, a key part of the future of the Mediterranean and of Europe is at stake.

13

MASSOUD LIVES!

Afghanistan, September 2020

The explosion occurred a few hours ago. A suicide car bomb. Double-parked on the shopping street of the Taimani neighborhood in the north part of Kabul. And when the convoy passed carrying Vice President Amrullah Saleh, a man known for his anti-Taliban militancy, the kamikaze driver pulled up alongside Saleh's armored car and detonated. The damage? Ten dead. Fifteen wounded. The vice president was spared, but left with burns to his hands and face. And within a hundred-meter radius, a chaos of twisted steel, felled power pylons, exploded gas canisters—and swarms of ordinary people screaming, coughing, fleeing the clouds of black smoke that hinted at a second explosion and caused people to abandon cars stuck in the ensuing traffic jam. Thank you, Taliban. A fine affirmation of the commitment you made in advance of the peace talks that will begin tomorrow in Doha to cease what you have the temerity to call "the fighting." Anger from Ahmad Muslem Hayat, who served as head security officer under the legendary Commander Ahmad Shah Massoud and had just returned from London to protect us in the course of this reporting. Hayat takes in the scene of the overwhelmed police; encourages the impoundment crews that are using cranes to remove abandoned vehicles; lends a hand to a rescue team as it pulls from the wreckage a waxy-skinned child whose breathing is a death rattle. "The same old story," growls the man who has gone through forty years of Afghan war and slaughter. "They're too cowardly to claim the attack; they'll pin it on al-Qaeda or on the Pakistani Lashkar-e-Taiba or the Haqqani group; but all those are the Taliban's beards – put that in your article!"

* * *

Who is Taliban? Who isn't? In a Kabul groaning under the weight of refugees, where foreigners haven't been seen in the street since Trump's summer announcement of the American withdrawal, what are the borders of the gray area in which a human bomb can pass unnoticed, like a fish in home waters? No one can say. We were told this the night before by Saad Mohseni, the founder of the Moby Media Group and the TOLOnews television channel that is the pride of the free media in Afghanistan and whose ultra-modern studios are sure to be one of the Taliban's first targets upon their return. Carnage like today's – or like that which occurred on May 12 in the Dasht-e-Barchi neighborhood, tearing apart a maternity hospital operated by Doctors without Borders and killing twenty-four, including three babies – can and will occur, he says, anywhere at any time. Through the window of my vehicle, I see an agitated man who, noticing us, makes the gesture of slitting his throat. A ragged peddler sitting on the sidewalk beside a pile of cell phones, padlocks, and old watches pretends to train a gun on our convoy. Another, hardly more than a boy, seeing that we're photographing him, spits in our direction. For the entire time we're driving, Commander Hayat clutches the Kalashnikov lying between him and the driver. Then, seeing that the traffic is blocked and we're no longer moving forward, he suggests we go the rest of the way on foot. It's September 9, the anniversary of Massoud's assassination nineteen years ago. And I have come to this downtown neighborhood to try to find the house where, in 1992, I had accompanied him on a visit to a wounded member of the Mujahideen. He was minister of defense at the time. And his old enemy, radical Islamist Gulbuddin Hekmatyar, was shelling the city from the hills.

* * *

I go from house to house, guided by a memory as vague as a dream, showing occupants an old photo of the nation's hero on my telephone. As we move farther away from the artery and into the maze of dusty, twisting streets of this Pashtun neighborhood, where wild grass grows in inner courtyards before the lanes reach dead ends imposed by bulky modern buildings, the people seem less hostile and, curiously, rather happy about "Massoud Day," even though it honors a Tajik. "You'll find the house you're looking for over there, just after the bazaar," we're told by a grandfatherly figure who recalls a neighbor whom Minister Massoud, "wearing a long white coat," had in fact come to comfort in midwinter, accompanied by a few bodyguards. "No, it's down there," corrects the *kalantar,* the neighborhood council head, whom someone had roused from a nap in the back of his lapis lazuli shop at the top of a shaky iron stairway. But it is a *kohnajrv,* a junk dealer, who ultimately leads us—through a labyrinth of shirts, tunics, and military trousers of every description hung on laundry lines—to what was the residence of Mola

Shams but where a commercial center is now sprouting up. I do not have time to learn more about the fate of the wounded Mujahideen fighter because our surroundings have become more worrisome, if almost imperceptibly. While skirting an open sewer, we come upon the severed head of a cat that seems to be taunting us. We pass adolescents with drugged-out looks. Women encased in burqas. And an informer comes to tell Commander Hayat that people are beginning to wonder about the foreigner who is asking impertinent questions.

* * *

I lived in the French embassy in the early months of 2002, after Jacques Chirac named me special envoy and asked me to prepare a proposal on a possible French contribution to rebuilding war-torn Afghanistan and, to be blunt, eradicating the Taliban. Twenty years later, where do we stand? The good news is that France has a strong ambassador, David Martinon, who spares no effort to convince the Afghans that it would be suicidal, on the eve of the negotiations in Doha, to yield to Islamist blackmail. The bad news is that his determination was not enough to prevent the secret release last night of the two motorcycle-mounted henchmen who, in the midst of a Kabul-scale traffic jam, gunned down Bettina Goislard, a young French aid worker, in Ghazni in 2003. More bad news is that since the truck-bomb attack against the embassy that caused two hundred deaths right in the middle of the Green Zone three years ago, the lovely white residence that we used to enter and exit without a second thought has become a besieged fortress protected by a complex of walls, sliding metal gates, concrete blocks, grates, and watchtowers in which the courageous ambassador and the twenty-four members of the elite French counterterrorist unit who protect him live in a state of war. It is hard not to think of the happy, almost joyous, atmosphere of the lunches that Gilles Hertzog and I hosted, on the same cheerful embassy grounds, for the same governors and military leaders, then young, that Martinon convenes on September 11. Karim Khalili, for example, is still the governor of Bamiyan province. He still has the same round face, with scarcely a trace of age, which his white, manicured beard is designed to toughen up. He continues to believe that, at the foot of the cliffs from which the Buddhas vandalized by the Taliban guarded the valley, a third, recumbent, Buddha lies buried, waiting only to be exhumed by DAFA, the French archaeological delegation in Afghanistan. But the difference is that, then, he was convinced that the Taliban had lost. Whereas today . . .

* * *

Abdullah Abdullah is the other president of Afghanistan. Not the vice president. The rival president. The one who contests the victory of Ashraf Ghani in the 2019 elections and took to bombarding him with vengeful inter-palatial communiqués. To shut him up, Ghani appointed him to head the delegation responsible for negotiating with the Taliban. But tonight, hosting us for dinner in his family home in Karte Parwan, he is not the Western-suited diplomat who will leave tomorrow for Doha. Instead, he is the resistance fighter clad in the traditional *salwar kameez* whom I met thirty years ago in the Panjshir Valley, where he was one of Commander Massoud's bravest lieutenants. He ends the evening taking us through room after room, the most striking features of which are the walls of photos of himself and his leader, young, in combat against the Soviets. Lost in reverie, he says little. He almost doesn't bother to correct me when the shadows in the room, the graininess of a photo, or the undeniable resemblance of the two men cause me to confuse the two faces. After a time, I break the silence: "Abdullah, my friend, what are you going to say to the Taliban? What might be your opening words? Where are your red lines? And can one really negotiate with people who, nineteen years ago, sent two fake journalists armed with a rigged camera to assassinate Massoud?" Abdullah remains evasive, murmuring that the country can't take any more, that forty years of war have exhausted it, and that we have to give peace a chance. Then, collecting himself and seeming to be filled with an ancient rage, he says, "Do you know that those dogs stalled for a month? That the whole operation was supposed to have gone down much earlier than it did? And that it was the commander himself, at the last minute, when the phony journalists thought it was never going to happen, who remembered about them and decided to grant them that fatal interview?" Abdullah's other face. The one that I know will not yield tomorrow in Qatar.

* * *

Here we are in Panjshir. The Afghan security services being full of double agents, the news of our movement leaked. So now it's battle stations on pro-Taliban social networks. And along the hundred kilometers of road that cross the Shomali Plain, which the Afghan army has trouble controlling, enemy checkpoints are a possibility. We called Saad Mohseni, who had introduced us the night before to the minister of defense and, right then and there, secured the use of a helicopter for us. Is it the same Mi-17 in which we traveled long ago with Massoud from Dushanbe, the capital of Tajikistan, to his advance posts in Jangalak, on the banks of the Panjshir River? It has the same too-rigid fuselage that, during turbulence, shudders along its entire length. The same sort of crew members testing the turbines, and then testing them again, before taking off and assuming their positions behind gun turrets trained on earthen mounds that, in the haze, look like enemy positions. It's the same cockpit with the same chock pulled up at the last minute on which Massoud had sat and prayed as we flew through the passes of the Hindu Kush. And what certainly has not changed is the landscape that greets us on landing, one of cubical houses, brick ovens, colorful walled orchards, the Panjshir River glistening under the last of the morning mist – in short, the village of Jangalak to which I arrived with Ahmad Shah Massoud and where today I find waiting to greet me . . . Ahmad Massoud. His son. His spitting image. The nine-year-old whom I can picture carrying into the family library the set of De Gaulle's war memoirs that I had brought as a gift for his father and who, twenty-two years later – with his *pakol* cap, well-groomed beard, and serious almond-shaped eyes – appears to be his reincarnation.

* * *

I ask him to tell me about the legendary father whom he resembles to such a startling degree. He tells me how he had dreamed of being the bravest of the brave once he reached manhood. How, while waiting for that time, he had brought his father his evening tea and helped him untie his shoes when he returned from the front. About this house, which his father had built but was able to occupy only for the last two weeks of his short life. About the garden that his father designed and planted with an artfulness worthy of the Babur Moguls. About his father's insect phobia and the odd morning toward the end, after the river had flooded, when he was found collecting drowning beetles and placing them safely on stones. The last supper . . . The last bunch of grapes that, on the day of his last departure, he had wanted to enjoy with his boy . . . "Is it really the last, Father? You mean the last of the season, right?" Yes, his father said to reassure him. But his son's young and deep soul understood that he had meant something different. The son's soul sensed, on that day of the last good-bye, his father's unwonted way of coming back for one more hug, of leaving again, and returning once more. And finally he tells about the moment of his father's death, of which I've never read a truly reliable account. His son recounts it to me as we cross the bridge where they used to walk: the commander's handsome face riddled with bomb shards, his chest crushed, one eye blown out, a leg severed – killed almost immediately; except, contrary to what has been said, he had the superhuman strength to call two guards spared by the explosion and order them to raise him by the shoulder blades; and there, standing upright for the last time, he recited the *shahadah,* the prayer of the dying.

* * *

But Massoud the younger, despite his overwhelming filial devotion, did not invite me here to dwell on stories of the past. Almost immediately we head toward Abshar, seventy kilometers east, where the Taliban last week launched an unprecedented attack on Panjshir. I watch him in the midst of his officers, some of them old enough to have served his father, and all now on alert.

While he inspects their positions and exhorts them to hold fast, I observe the authority that radiates from his still-boyish face. I listen as he explains to them that he wanted neither to go into politics nor to participate in these bizarre peace negotiations, because his place is here with them, at the gates of what was and, if the fighting resumes, what must absolutely remain the inviolate sanctuary of free Afghanistan. And when, at the bottom of a vertiginous gorge from which one can hear only the bells of a distant herd, the time comes for the shooting contest, which his father also used to propose to his guests, the evidence speaks for itself. The target is a white pebble placed on a ridge of ochre stone seventy meters away in the shadow of the folds of the mountain. Although my own performance with an assault rifle has hardly improved over the intervening years, he takes aim three times and three times, to the cheers of his companions, scores a bull's-eye. Ahmad Massoud is an elite marksman. He possesses the skill and, perhaps, the composure of the warriors immemorial of the Afghan mountains. Not to mention the fact that this young man of letters, who, after the murder of his father, was exfiltrated to Iran and then quickly to London, became a brilliant cadet at Sandhurst, where for two centuries the British army's elites have been trained.

* * *

We move on to the marble mausoleum in which his father rests, where other officers await him, including, on this first Friday after Massoud Day, delegations that have come from Kandahar and Jalalabad to celebrate the memory of the Lion of Panjshir. And there (first before hundreds of peasant soldiers whose tunics shine in the blinding light, and then in the park of wrecked tanks that commemorates one of the boldest acts of the war between the Mujahideen and the Soviets), I glimpse yet another side of this prodigious young man. He is eloquent, an inspired, lyrical orator, speaking not only in the name of his Panjshiri brothers but now on behalf of the entire

Afghan nation. And saluting France, which, in the darkest hour, never abandoned this people of potters, nomads, shepherds, and poets. "Twenty years have passed," I begin, when he gives me the floor.

> I return with a heavy heart to these mountains still mourning a commander whose cowardly assassination, not far from here, opened the new century like the prologue to a funeral. But I am discovering that the embers of freedom still burn in this valley. I understand that – thanks to his companions of that time, to his spiritual children of today, and to his son by blood and soul who did me the honor of asking me here, to stand at his side – the memory of the commander continues to live in these mountains. We are in debt to the aptly named Ahmad Massoud for keeping the promises of his father. We are grateful that he stands as the same sentry guarding the heart of this land, a sentry whose name shall be engraved in the book of courage and the greatness of man. Tomorrow, whatever the outcome of the encounter with the Taliban, whatever the bitter fruits of compromise with the fanatics, and however appalling the treachery of your allies, who have chosen to lose this war and to sacrifice you, I shall bear witness that here, at the base of these mountains, the fight for freedom resumed – indeed, it never ceased. In the darkness of these times, there is good news. A new Lion of Panjshir is born.

* * *

Finally we return to his childhood home, where we take a last tea on the long garnet sofas facing the river where his father would meditate. "I love three things in this world," he begins. "Books.

Gardens. And the astronomy I learned at King's College London before entering Sandhurst, which instilled in me the habit of looking each night at the sky and its constellations. This means that, contrary to what you said earlier at the mausoleum, I was not cut out for political action. But someone had to pick up the torch. The hope my glorious father embodied could not be allowed to die out. So, yes, for that reason, and for that reason alone, I am ready to take over."

Before leaving, I ask him three questions. Whether he is prepared to declare, in the charter of the movement he has created, that being the son of his father is not enough and that his crown truly belongs not to him but to the people of the Mujahideen. Whether he is willing to announce that he seeks the votes of the Afghan nation for the sole purpose of launching reforms that the country's feudal lords never wanted, and that he will then return to deciphering the meaning of the stars. And whether there are principles – starting with women's rights – on which no peacemaker will be permitted to compromise as long as he, Massoud, lives. To each of these questions he answers affirmatively. And he does so in the same clear, resonant voice his father used twenty-two years ago when, amid the gathering storm, he accepted my invitation to come to Paris. Have we come to that point again? Might Massoud the Second be a new knight determined to put in check the warlords who, in the face of the Taliban peril, are only the hulks of their former selves? Is it possible that, in this last moment of the confrontations on which our joint fate hinges, we have a protagonist, at least one, who will definitely say no to obscurantism, to rule by murder, and to the spirit of resignation? I fervently hope so.

EPILOGUE

Often when I leave on a reporting trip my children and others close to me worry. "Aren't you afraid?" they ask.

This, too, deserves a word of clarification – and this will be the last, I promise.

Yes, of course I was afraid when, as a young man, I found myself thrown into the firing range of the war in Bangladesh, where death was everywhere, struck haphazardly, and exploded in the middle of a crowd.

Of course I was afraid when, in the Angolan sky approaching Moxico, the pilot announced that because missile launchers might begin firing at any moment the only solution was to go into a nosedive and to wait until the last minute to pull back on the stick and bring the nose up.

Of course I was afraid – only an imbecile would not have been – when I would leave the Holiday Inn in Sarajevo or the runway of the besieged airport, or was running along the bank of the Miljacka to the right of the presidential palace, and I was always exposed for part of the way (ten, fifty, or a hundred meters). And there may have been a Serb sniper up in the hills sitting on his collapsible stool next to his cooler and watching me like an insect through his scope. If he fired, he was not likely to miss.

And I would have been an idiot not to have been afraid when alone, unprotected, in the streets of Karachi; alone, with a handful of Peshmerga who had erred into the outskirts of Fazliya and, without allied air support, had to beat back an assault by the Islamic State; alone, again, in the Taliban-infested Chicken Street quarter of Kabul for one of the reports in this collection, as I struck out in search of the house of Mola Shams, the wounded Mujahideen, and his daughter, Homa, the brilliant young journalist whom I had recruited in 2002 to write for *Les Nouvelles de Kaboul* (Homa later obtained an advance on her salary to buy barbiturates to kill herself because she, a Dari, loved a Pashtun); alone when, in Tarhouna, Libya, I stumbled in among a furious horde howling "Death to the Jew," and shooting at me; alone when, in the Qara Chokh mountains of Iraqi Kurdistan, strapped into a harness so as not to fall, I descended a steep cliff—right down to the entrance to an ISIS grotto.

So?

So, obviously, in such circumstances, one takes precautions.

There are hothead reporters like Paul Marchand, the mysterious young man everyone talked about in Sarajevo between July 1992 and October 1993, whose risky behavior included walking a tightrope between the half-destroyed twin towers of downtown Sarajevo under the nose of the snipers in the hills. But for the most part, and certainly for me, the rule is to calculate, to reflect, to weigh every risk taken against the value of the alert that might be sounded by obtaining an original interview, observing a scene, or taking a photo that someone didn't want you to take.

Often, that's not enough.

It can be a step too far, as was the case for the American hero, Daniel Pearl, on the day before he was to return to the United States, when he was caught in a trap that al-Qaeda set for him in Karachi, a city crawling with jihadists specializing in beheadings.

Or the one photo too many for Tim Hetherington, the courageous photographer killed along with Chris Hondros in Misrata on April 20, 2011. He had just slipped through a hole in a building facade, where a rocket blast caught up with him.

But usually it is enough, and when you get the proportions right, when you have, as Aristotle recommended, properly balanced impulse and reason, enthusiasm and prudence, things go well: you return in the evening to the hotel or base camp; you read your notes; you take in the scents of the wind; you watch the rising tide of stars in the sky; you are content. And several days later, when your mission is accomplished, you will have done your job as a man and your duty as a brother. You return to your cherished research, to the book you're writing, to life.

Except that this explanation is not enough.

Neither I nor any of the war reporters I know would be capable of closing with a cool account of risks and precautions.

However reasonable one is, when one runs the risk of a sniper, a stray bullet, a blind rocket, or, as in sailing toward Misrata, a shelf of rock just under the water unseen by the ship's instruments, there is always a moment when from deep inside comes the more basic question of one's relationship with death – not that of others, not that of the forgotten victims whose story one has sworn to tell, but one's own.

That is the most difficult question.

The most basic but also the headiest one – because for each of us, reporter or not, voyager or not, it is the most intimate secret, the best concealed, the deepest of all the secrets we carry around with us – secret from others, as Michel Foucault said, but also from ourselves.

I know some who have spent a lifetime honing their doctrine, as Foucault himself did, staging the final meeting, planning to make it a play without an audience, one that will exist only for themselves but will count nonetheless, only to utter this childish phrase as he reaches the end: "Call Canguilhem, he knows how to die."

I know some who have lived with the certainty, as my other former professor, Jacques Derrida, did – that since the "I" is nothing but an artifact of language, a knot of Husserlian intentionalities, an empty point, a fold, they would rise to the moment, round the cape, ram it home. Even so, I am told, panic comes at the end, along with incredulity and a bewildered, guilty feeling.

Or, conversely, my anti-professor, Gilles Deleuze, whose philosophical opposition I encountered upon publishing *Barbarism with a Human Face,* and who would have been happy enough to see me abandon philosophy altogether. We were not yet enemies and would even have an occasional late-afternoon tea at the old bar at the Hotel Lutetia in Paris, talking of everything and nothing. Yes, nothing, in fact. "Death is nothing," he maintained. Just another arrangement of animal spirits and matter. Pasternak was wrong: it is death, not life, who is our sister. And, indeed, Deleuze died a death Deleuzian and Roman.

Or, conversely again, and sticking with famous, documented deaths and well-known secrets, there was Voltaire's strange death. A life spent defying it. Posing as the strong mind ("God? We greet each other but without saying a word!"). Setting a trap for death, taking it from behind, playing a clever game. If he could have, Voltaire would have had himself tested, vaccinated, every morning. He was one of those who thought that the Enlightenment, science, and medicine would defeat once and for all disease, evil, and death. A life spent policing the deathbeds of others. Some score well, such as Lady Pompadour, "who died like a philosopher"; others, not so well, such as La Fontaine ("died like a drunk") and Maupertuis ("between two Capuchin monks"). And after all that, when his time came, to be surrounded by a cook and a few visitors who had paid to see him die; to cry like a baby; to shout at his doctor, "I am abandoned by God and men! I'll give you half my fortune if you will give me six more months to live"; and, some say, to smear himself with his own excrement.

You just never know.

Never does one have a clear idea of the scene of one's death or the role one will play in it.

And one must be very careful, very modest – one must weigh one's words as one approaches these shores.

But having taken these precautions and understanding that the heart of the secret lies, as it so often does, in the hands of God, I know two or three things about death related to this book and to the questions it raises.

As a child, when I discovered *The Iliad* and *The Odyssey* through the wonderful French collection entitled *Contes et Légendes* (*Tales and Legends*), whose cover illustrations enchanted generations of girls and boys, I was convinced that my mother, like Thetis, had dipped me in the Styx. And I cunningly told myself that if I managed, once I was grown, to become one of those explorers or adventurers that I was just then discovering in the novels of Stevenson and Conrad, death would have to deploy a great deal of intelligence, ingenuity, and trickery to find the spot on me that hadn't been anointed with the water of invulnerability and love.

In adolescence, I was bowled over by a poem by Rainer Maria Rilke appearing in *Le Livre de la Pauvreté et de la Mort* that eerily foretold Foucault. In it, the poet prayed that each be given "his own death," the one and true death that sprang from "his own life" and "the fruit" of an existence that had been but "the bark and the leaf," an end he described as a "great death." And I remember later reading Rilke's *Notebooks of Malte Laurids Brigge,* and the emotion I felt when I reached the story of the grandfather's death – described by the author as a "great death."

I was skeptical of the whole Symbolist rapture business (Wagner, Isolde dying, flooded with light, on the corpse of her lover . . .) but never of the idea of a great death. I was enchanted that there might be, for each of us, whether vanquished or victor, humble or arrogant, sheep or wolf, a small death and a great death. Great death was the death of Danton or Jean Moulin. It was the death of the great captains who had waged a just war. It was the death of the infantrymen of the *Army of Shadows* who did not talk under torture. It was even the death of revolutionaries. And all that was part of the heroic conception that I had of life.

Here, too, time has passed.

And I stopped putting much stock in my youthful illusions.

(Although there was that moment in August 2011 in Martyrs' Square in Tripoli, filmed on a cell phone and included in *The Oath of Tobruk,* when firing broke out on all sides and something or someone told me that I did not need to quicken or slow my pace, everything would be fine, I am protected . . .)

But I have forged, in the place of these illusions, a set of convictions that make up a part of me, like those faces that we compose over time and, after forty years, wind up being responsible for.

For example, I believe that we must try – try, mind you – not to think too much about death, at least not until it is imminent.

There are two schools of thought.

To talk about it all the time, to converse with it, and hope thereby to tame it.

Or to forget about it, not prepare, nor put your papers in order, leave things hanging, and hope that death, too, will forget.

I am of the second school.

With, in my case, additional arguments.

The demand for decency with respect to distant others who do not have the luxury of taming anything because they know they will die like dogs ("worldless," Heidegger would say), and that death, that inviolable and sacred secret, will be stolen from them.

The wish to leave in peace those close to me, whose lives I spoil by haranguing them – in the manner of hypochondriacs, Doctor Knocks, and health and hygiene fanatics – on the subject of my certain death and its uncertain hour.

And next a dietary question, but this time for my own consumption: a life that thinks only of death, a life that does little beside prepare for death, a life in which we offer Asclepius roosters day and night, a life spent chasing after vaccines and then, when the vaccines arrive, worry that they may not be effective against each emerging variant, is an empty life, a life lived for nothing, a nihilistic life. Nietzsche said all that needs to be said on that subject.

I also believe that not everything is mortal, that not everything returns unto dust, and that there is something in a man's life that will live on after him.

I am not referring to his soul or his body. I am not one of those, like Sartre in his last interviews with Benny Lévy, who believes in the resurrection of the body.

I refer to his works.

I am talking about a man determined to accomplish something.

And I believe that, in a writer, a real one, one who works with his head and his hands, with his intelligence and his lungs, his wisdom and desire, one in whom body and soul contend, clash, and come to terms on a blank page, one who writes as if life and death depend on it, one who throws himself wholeheartedly, with all his might, into the books he writes, one who sweats blood and water (and I do not know, when one writes like this, whether he sweats more in doing the things or relating them) – I believe that, in such a writer, in that "terrible worker" (Rimbaud again), a singular chemistry is at work.

There are words, sometimes lines, in which something is deposited, something that is the writer without being him and yet being him eminently, even if it falls away from him and becomes a stranger to him, even if, as with Sartre, for example, he does not recognize himself in it and never rereads it. It is something issued from a form and matter that were his essence. It is, literally, the best of him.

As long as there are people, even just a few, to make a place in their heart for these words, these lines, I believe that the words will continue, without their author, after him, to live their life, to tremble on their stem, and, like fallen willow branches that begin growing again in a sheath of sand, to exist in the lives of others.

I believe that over the life that lives on, over the life that, emitting its own light, crosses space and time to take root in another life; over that satellite of life, that capsule of life, that life palpitating like a synthesized soul, aching like a missing limb, and lacking nothing but consciousness – I believe that over such a life death has no hold as long as there are ears to hear it and to divine the sound of the voice that breathed it.

Blessed by words, in a sense. Saved by the life of books. That is another conviction. And it reassures me.

And finally I believe that a life is not a life and does not make us accomplished people unless it is a little more than life and adheres to an idea, an ideal, a principle, or certain values that transcend it and raise it above itself.

"Liberty or death," said the French revolutionaries.

"Better to die standing than to live on one's knees" was the cry of the childhood heroes whom I still admire.

And that could be said of many others, less glorious or not glorious at all, untraceable, nameless: I believe there is in every woman and every man a passage to greatness, every single one, not only the great by their transcendental calling, such as kings, near-kings, artists, and writers.

I love life passionately and hope to love it still longer and better. But I know that it is worth nothing if it is not fed by the idea, not of a great death, but of a great life. And I believe the greatest of lives are those that – having resolved to leave a last word, not to death but to life – decide not to accept death when it prowls around those whom one loves or whom one has decided to protect.

I have never given much credence to all the stories of adrenaline, intense moments, and so on that are told about war reporters. I don't believe that skirting the abyss and, in so doing, leaving open an inner window on death boosts the gusto for life that one feels upon returning safe and sound. I believe even less in it since I have many times had the opposite experience of returning from a reporting trip in which I saw death close up, not my own but that of others, and had trouble resurfacing and resuming life as I had lived it before. But I think I know what I sought from all those distant voyages, those reporting adventures. What I was chasing is probably the exquisite diversity of my fellow man. But I also found in those lands that I frequented fifty years ago, twenty years ago, or a few months ago, lands where one is great not because one is born that way but because one has no other choice and cannot behave otherwise. I have found beautiful stories of resistance, struggle, goodness, and abnegation that I have never forgotten and that testify to a true love of life lived greatly.

It may be said that these convictions are vague and rhetorical and will not do me any good when the moment comes for me, too, to take my leave.

Maybe that's true.

But that's not the moment I'm talking about.

I'm talking about right now.

I'm talking about the moment when I land on the bush runway in Moxico.

The moment when I come back from Jazeera, in Somalia, by the same route because there is none other than the one I took coming in, and the chances are one in a hundred, one in ten, or one in two that the terrorists of al-Shabaab have laid a mine in the meantime.

The moment when I imagine – one's imagination always being the tool of last resort when pondering fear and ways to dispel it – my body wounded like Jean Hatzfeld's in Bosnia, tortured like Daniel Pearl's in Karachi, or sick, as I was in Bangladesh.

And at such moments, I don't think it's just idle chatter to say that that's how I operate.

I don't play melancholy like Rilke.

I no longer pose as a protégé of Malraux.

I don't cry like Verdi or preach like a philosopher or priest, exhorting myself not to be afraid . . .

I am not even audacious, knowing that audacity can be a form of unconsciousness, a way to close one's eyes on the real, silence the mind, and replace it with bodily activity.

On the contrary, my eyes are open.

They are open more widely than they ever have been since they are no longer distracted by conceptualizing death or papering it over, as are the eyes of those who make a habit of thinking about death.

And it is this collection of lucidities and certitudes, this viaticum of beliefs and, to use the term one last time, reflexes, that crystallize in me, comfort me, anchor my determination, and cause me to move forward – on my own, without a guardian angel, believing that if risks there be, they are noble risks that must be taken.

And if the reader is still not convinced; if he objects that these certitudes reek of swagger and terrors not truly overcome; if he insists that they are, as we would have said at the École Normale

Supérieure, rhetorical, badly constructed, or too composed; if he sees in them a remnant of the aesthetically inclined games of adolescence, so be it: at least it will prove that what makes a man immortal is his Achilles' heel.

INDEX

Surnames starting with "al-" or "el" are alphabetized by the principal part of the name.